THE NEWEST NINJA FOODI MAX GRILL AND AIR FRYER COOKBOOK 2024

1001-Day Ninja Air Fryer Recipes for Your Whole Family to Fry, Bake, Broil, Grill, Roast

TABLE OF CONTENTS

SANDWICHES & BURGERS RECIPES 76

BEEF, PORK & LAMB RECIPES 81

INTRODUCTION

WHAT FOODS ARE BEST FOR THE AIR FRYER?

Now that you have decided on the best air fryer for you, the fun part is actually putting it to use! You can pretty much put any food into your air fryer to cook however, just like other kitchen appliances, there are certain foods that cook better than others. I have noted of what works best in the air fryer after trying out different recipes and here are my findings.

FROZEN FOODS

The original concept of the air fryer was made to reheat and rapidly cook frozen foods. I found that it does this well. All the food was cooked to perfection with no oil added. The food was cooked right through without any burning on the outside. Some of the frozen foods that I cooked and the results:

- French fries: Comes out crispier and crunchier than the oven.
- Mini pizza's: Toppings are juicy and the base is crunchy.
- Chicken nuggets: Outer layer is crispy and chicken inside is tender.
- Vegetable croquettes: Crispy on the outside and soft on the inside.
- Meatballs: Outer layer is crispy and meat inside is tender.
- Chicken wings: Perfectly grilled on the outside and juicy on the inside.
- Fish sticks: Crunchy on the outside and soft on the inside.
- Chicken breasts: Soft and tender on the inside.
- Fish fillets: Melts in your mouth.

The only thing to be aware of is that smaller air fryers might not fit a medium to large size pizzas. Therefore you need to consider what types of food you will be cooking regularly when deciding on your air fryer size.

VEGETABLES

Most of the vegetables that you love can be cooked in the air fryer. However, depending on how you like you like them done, some vegetables are better in the air fryer than others. It was noted that some vegetables comes out soft and juicy while others comes out crispy and crunchy. I also noticed that they do seem to retain more of their nutritional value as the vegetables were not overcooked.

Soft and juicy vegetables when air fried included:
- Mushrooms
- Zucchini
- Butternut squash
- Cherry tomatoes
- Aubergine
- Bell Pepper

Crispy and crunchy vegetables when air fried included:
- Cauliflower
- Brussels sprouts
- Asparagus

Vegetables that I am still trying to perfect with the air fryer:
- Broccoli: They are too crunchy for me and when I tried to increase the time, they get a bit burnt.
- Sweet Potato: The outside gets a bit burnt if I want the inside cooked through.

MEATS

Cooking meat with the air fryer is a delight as you don't have to worry about the meat being burnt or undercooked, especially uneven pieces of meat. The only trick is to get the right temperature and timer set to have a perfectly cooked piece of meat.The first step would be the user manual of your air fryer. Then you can refer to any cookbooks or any other recipes that you can come across. Some air fryers even have preset programs that you can use as a beginner.Once you have got an estimated temperature or timer you can manually adjust the elements up or down to suit the way you like to have your meat. As we all have different taste buds and preferences, it may take you a few tries before you find your perfect settings.

In saying this, I have listed below some of my findings while cooking my meat in the air fryer.

- *Chicken*: With the <u>small air fryers</u> the best chicken pieces to cook would be the evenly shaped pieces like chicken breasts and chicken tenderloins as the basket size is smaller. The <u>family sized</u> and <u>extra large</u> air fryers can accommodate a whole chicken depending on the model and capacity air fryer you have. Chicken generally comes out tender and juicy.

- *Beef*: Steaks and kebabs are done fairly well as it can be done medium to well done simply by adjusting the temperature or timer settings. You have control of the process. Most air fryers even allows you to slide the basket out during the cooking process to check on your food midway.

- *Lamb*: Steaks and lamb chops are done perfectly when air fried as they are juicy and tender. Lamb rack , however, proved to be tricky depending on the size of your air fryer. For small to medium air fryers it is recommended to cut it into smaller pieces for best results.

SEAFOOD

I found grilling seafood in the air fryer keeps most of the juices inside therefore I could taste more of the seafood flavor. Naturally, fresh seafood is always best if you want to taste the seafood flavors.

I found that seafood is cooked faster in the air fryer and the flesh is soft and tender. Some of the things to note are:

- Prawns and Lobster: Grilling them in the shell really brought out there natural flavors.

- Fish: Fillets had the best outcome with the air fryer as they fit in the basket and there is still enough room for the air circulation to cook them evenly. Even with salmon fillets where the middle are thicker and the edges are thinner, the air fryer is able to cook them evenly. Grilling whole fish is also great in the bigger air fryers but not recommended for smaller air fryers as you would need to cut your fish in half.

- Scallops: Few minutes in the air fryer and they come out tender, juicy and full of flavor.

You can put most food types into the air fryer for cooking. The trick is to get the settings right for each specific type of food. This comes with trying different recipes and noting down what you like and don't like. Over time, you would have discovered what works best to suit your taste buds. Hope that you can have as much fun as I am cooking with air fryer!

FAVORITE AIR FRYER RECIPES

Air Fryer Hot Pockets

Servings: 2
Cooking Time: 11 Minutes

Ingredients:

- 2 frozen Hot Pockets (any variety)

Directions:

1. Preheat your air fryer to 350 degrees.
2. Place Hot Pockets inside the air fryer without the crisper sleeve and cook for 11-13 minutes, until heated thoroughly.
3. Carefully remove them from the air fryer and place the Hot Pocket crispers back on and let cool.
4. Enjoy! Be careful as the first bite may still be hot.

NOTES
How to Heat Up a Hot Pocket Faster
Preheat air fryer to 400 degrees.
Microwave the Hot Pocket for 60 seconds in the crisper sleeve.
Carefully remove the Hot Pocket from the microwave and remove from the crisper sleeve.
Heat the Hot Pocket in the air fryer for 3-4 minutes until warmed thoroughly. Then let cool for at least 5 minutes. The Hot Pocket may still be hot upon the first bite.

Pear Wontons

Ingredients:

- 2 Bartlett pears
- 1/2 cup honey
- 1 tsp ground cinnamon
- 1 package wonton wrappers
- Water, for sealing
- 2 Tbsp unsalted butter, melted
- 1/4 cup mascarpone cheese
- 1 Tbsp honey
- 1/2 tsp ground cinnamon

Directions:

1. Core and chop the pears into small bite size pieces and add to a medium bowl.
2. Add about 1/2 cup honey and 1 tsp cinnamon to the pears and mix. Set aside.
3. Assemble the wonton by adding a teaspoon of the pears to the center.
4. Dip your fingers into some water and wet all four edges.
5. Fold into a triangle shape. Press and pinch the edges together to seal.
6. Continue this process until all the pears or wonton wrappers are gone.
7. Fill your air fryer basket, making sure not to overlap them.
8. Melt 2 Tablespoons of butter and brush on top of each wonton.
9. Air fry at 350F for minutes, or until crispy.
10. While those are cooking, make the dip. Mix the mascarpone cheese, 1 Tbsp honey and 1/2 tsp cinnamon together.
11. You can simply dip these into the mascarpone cheese mixture or you can elevate them by adding a scoop onto each wonton and top with chopped pecans!
12. ENJOY!

Air Fryer Jalapeno Poppers

Servings: 4
Cooking Time: 8 Minutes

Ingredients:

- 8 jalapeno peppers
- 6 ounces herb & garlic cream cheese or Boursin
- ¾ cup sharp cheddar cheese shredded
- 4 tablespoons bacon bits or 4 slices bacon cooked and crumbled
- ⅓ cup Panko breadcrumbs
- 1 tablespoon butter melted

Directions:

1. Preheat the air fryer to 400°F.
2. In a small bowl combine Panko, bacon and melted butter. Set aside.
3. Slice the jalapenos in half lengthwise and scrape out the seeds. Use gloves or wash your hands well afterward.
4. Combine cream cheese and shredded cheddar together in a bowl. Fill jalapenos with the cheese mixture.
5. Sprinkle each jalapeno with the Panko and bacon topping, lightly pressing to adhere.
6. Air fry for 7-9 minutes or until cheese is melted and jalapenos are tender crisp.
7. Cool at least 5 minutes before serving.

NOTES

It is recommended to wear gloves while working with the jalapenos.

Slow Cooker - Green Chile Queso Dip Recipe W Jalapeño

Servings: 8
Cooking Time: 2 Hours

Ingredients:

- FOR THE QUESO DIP:
- 16 oz. (453g) Velveeta Cheese , cut into 1" cubes for quick melting
- 15 oz. (425g) canned chili (no beans)
- 4 oz. (113g) canned diced green chiles
- 1 fresh jalapeno pepper , minced (optional)
- 1/2 teaspoon kosher salt , or to taste
- 1 teaspoon ground cumin
- 2 teaspoons smoked paprika
- 2 teaspoons chili powder
- 1 teaspoon ground chipotle powder
- 1/2 teaspoon ground cayenne pepper
- 1 cup (240ml) Half & Half
- OPTIONS FOR SERVING:
- tortilla chips (preferred!)
- Potato Chips
- Crackers
- Veggies

Directions:

1. In slow cooker, add all the ingredients and stir together well: Velveeta cheese, chili, diced green chiles, fresh jalapeño, sea salt, ground cumin, smoked paprika, chili powder, chipotle powder, ground cayenne pepper and Half and Half.
2. Cook on low for about 3 hours or High for about 2 hours. Stir occasionally to make sure all the cheese melts.

NOTE

Cooking time will vary depending on the size of slow cooker you are using. If you are using larger slow cookers, more of the dip will be spread across the slow cooker so the cheese will melt faster. Smaller slow cookers will take longer to melt and cook the dip. Check the dip each hour, stir and you determine when it's ready to serve.

Serve the yummy queso dip with tortilla chips or the other options.

Eggplant Pizza Recipe

Servings: 12
Cooking Time: 22 Minutes

Ingredients:

- 1 large eggplant
- 1 1/2 tbsp olive oil
- 1/2 cup (120 g) tomato sauce (e.g. marinara or pizza sauce)
- 2 garlic cloves minced
- Salt and pepper to taste
- 1 tsp dried oregano
- 3/4 cup (90 g) vegan mozzarella (I used homemade)
- 1/2 cup (90 g) cherry tomatoes halved
- 1/4 cup (45 g) olives sliced
- Fresh basil chopped for garnish

Directions:

1. You can watch the short video for visual instructions.

2. Preheat the oven to 425 °F (220 °C) and line a baking sheet with parchment paper.

3. Slice the eggplant horizontally into ½-inch (1 cm) thick slices. Brush a little olive oil on each side of the slices and place them on the lined baking sheet.

4. Sprinkle with a little salt, pepper, and the half amount of dried oregano. Bake in the oven for 15 minutes.

5. Mix the tomato sauce with the minced garlic, salt, pepper, and the remaining oregano.

6. After 15 minutes, remove the eggplant slices from the oven, and top them with the tomato sauce, vegan mozzarella, and any toppings you like (I used cherry tomatoes and olives).

7. Bake for a further 10-12 minutes. Garnish with fresh basil and enjoy!

NOTES

Slice them evenly: So the eggplant pizzas all cook at an even rate.

Don't underbake the eggplant: Eggplant can be spongy and rubbery when not cooked enough.

Don't skip the pre-roast: The first 15 minutes of roasting time are needed to bring out some water from the eggplant slices and get it to the correct texture.

Don't use too many toppings: Otherwise, the eggplant pizza might turn out soggy.

Read the blog post for more tips, FAQs, and serving suggestions.

Air-fryer Sausage Pizza

Servings: 4

Ingredients:
- 1 loaf (1 pound) frozen bread dough, thawed
- 1 cup pizza sauce
- 1/2 pound bulk Italian sausage, cooked and drained
- 1-1/3 cups shredded part-skim mozzarella cheese
- 1 small green pepper, sliced into rings
- 1 teaspoon dried oregano
- Crushed red pepper flakes, optional

Directions:

1. On a lightly floured surface, roll and stretch dough into four 4-in. circles. Cover; let rest for 10 minutes.

2. Preheat air fryer to 400°. Roll and stretch each dough into a 6-in. circle. Place 1 crust on greased tray in air-fryer basket. Carefully spread with 1/4 cup pizza sauce, 1/3 cup sausage, 1/3 cup cheese, a fourth of the green pepper rings and a pinch of oregano. Cook until crust is golden brown, 6-8 minutes. If desired, sprinkle with red pepper flakes. Repeat with remaining ingredients.

Air Fryer Mini Pizzas

Servings: 4
Cooking Time: 4 Minutes

Ingredients:
- 1 can Grand's biscuits
- 1 cup marinara sauce
- 10 pepperoni slices
- 8 ounces mozzarella cheese shredded
- 1/2 teaspoon olive oil

Directions:

1. Open the package of biscuits and separate each biscuit into two layers.

2. Roll each piece of biscuit out into a 4-inch circle of dough.

3. Top each piece of dough with about 1 teaspoon of marinara sauce.

4. Add pepperoni to the sauce and put freshly shredded mozzarella cheese on top of the pizzas.

5. Spray the air fryer basket with non-stick cooking spray, olive oil spray, or line with parchment paper.

6. Carefully place 2-4 of the mini pizzas into the air fryer basket, leaving an inch or more of space between each pizza.

7. Air fry the mini pizzas at 400° Fahrenheit (200 degrees Celcius) for 4 minutes, or until the pizzas have a golden brown crispy crust. Add additional cooking time if needed.

8. Carefully remove the air fried biscuit pizzas from the air fryer basket and allow them to cool slightly on a cooling rack.

9. Repeat the cooking process with the remaining pizzas.

10. Serve immediately.

NOTES

This recipe was made with a 1700 watt basket style Cosori 5.8 air fryer. All air fryers cook a little differently. You may need to adjust the cooking time according to your brand of air fryer. The size and power output of your air fryer may be different, and you should check on your dish frequently the first time you make it to see if it is cooking faster or slower and if you need to add or take away cook time.

Garnish the pizzas with all of your favorite pizza toppings and serve sprinkled with fresh parmesan cheese and fresh chopped basil.

Play with additional toppings such as ground beef, mushrooms, peppers, pineapple, and more.

Flaky Caprese Pinwheels

Servings: 8

Ingredients:

- 3 tablespoons of tomato sauce
- 1 sheet puff pastry, thawed
- 2 tablespoons basil pesto
- 1½ cups mozzarella, shredded
- ½ teaspoon ground black pepper
- Items Needed
- Parchment paper

Directions:

1. Spread the tomato sauce onto the top half of the puff pastry and basil pesto onto the bottom, leaving a ¼ inch of the edge bare.
2. Spread the mozzarella on top of the tomato sauce on the puff pastry.
3. Roll the puff pastry tightly starting from the top toward yourself until you get to the bottom.
4. Halve the roll, then cut the halves into quarters. You should end up with 8 pinwheels.
5. Select the Preheat function on the Air Fryer, adjust temperature to 370°F, then press Start/Pause.
6. Line the air fryer basket with parchment paper.

7. Place the pin wheels into the preheated air fryer, leaving ½-inch spaces between each pinwheel.
8. Sprinkle the ground black pepper on top of the wheels.
9. Set temperature to 370°F and time to 15 minutes, then press Start/Pause.
10. Remove the pinwheels when done, then serve.

Spicy Sticky Winglets

Ingredients:

- ¼ cup sweet chili
- ¼ cup coke
- 1 tbsp soy sauce
- ½ tsp chili flakes
- 1 cinammon stick
- ½ tsp blended black pepper or regular freshly cracked black pepper with a pinch of cayenne Pepper
- Pinch of salt
- For extra sauce, double above measurements.

Directions:

1. Place your wings in the airfyer tray and airfry for 15 minutes at 180 °C (the airfryer will prompt you to turn the wings halfway through cooking). While wings are cooking, prepare your sauce by combining all your sauce ingredients in a bowl. Set your Instant Pot on a saute mode, add your sauce combination, mix well and allow to simmer. Allow sauce to simmer for about 2 minutes, once thickened remove cinnamon stick and set aside.
2. Once wings are cooked, transfer to a large bowl and pour the sauce over the wings (reserve a ¼ of the sauce for dipping). Toss wings in sauce and ensure that they are generously coated.
3. Optional: serve with a dusting of toasted sesame seeds and chopped chives and enjoy with a squeeze of lime, extra sauce reserved for dipping and a side of your choice.

Sweet Potato Wedges

Servings: 6
Cooking Time: 23 Minutes

Ingredients:

- 3 medium sweet potatoes
- 2 tablespoons extra virgin olive oil
- 1 teaspoon kosher salt plus additional for serving
- 1 teaspoon garlic powder
- 1/4 teaspoon chipotle chile powder use less if sensitive to spice or omit
- ¼ teaspoon ground black pepper
- ¼ teaspoon dried rosemary

Directions:

1. Place a rack in the center of your oven and preheat the oven to 450 degrees F.
2. Scrub and dry the sweet potatoes. Peel them if you like (I leave the peels on sweet potatoes).
3. Cut each sweet potato in half lengthwise. Cut each half into 3 or 4 long spears (so you will have 6 to 8 wedges per potato). Each spear should be about ¾-inch to 1-inch wide; the most important thing is to cut them as uniform in size as you can so that they bake evenly.
4. Place the spears on a rimmed baking sheet and drizzle with the oil.
5. In a small bowl, stir together the salt, garlic powder, chipotle chile powder, black pepper, and rosemary. Sprinkle over the potatoes and toss to coat, ensuring the wedges are evenly coated with the oil and spices.
6. Arrange the sweet potato wedges into a single layer, being careful that the wedges do not touch (if your pan is crowded and they are touching, divide the wedges between two baking sheets and bake in the upper and lower thirds of the oven instead).
7. Bake the sweet potato wedges for 15 minutes, then turn over with a spatula. Return the pan to the oven and bake for another 5 to 10 minutes, until lightly browned and tender when pierced with a fork.
8. Turn the oven to broil. Broil the sweet potatoes for 3 to 5 minutes, until they are crisped at the edges to your liking (watch carefully so that they do not burn). Remove from the oven and immediately sprinkle with a pinch of additional salt. Enjoy!

NOTES

TO STORE: Refrigerate sweet potato wedges in an airtight storage container for up to 4 days.

TO REHEAT: Rewarm leftovers on a baking sheet in the oven at 350 degrees F.

TO FREEZE: Freeze wedges in an airtight freezer-safe storage container for up to 3 months. Let thaw overnight in the refrigerator before reheating.

Air Fryer Frozen Taquitos

Servings: 4
Cooking Time: 6 Minutes

Ingredients:

- 8 taquitos
- salsa & sour cream for serving optional

Directions:

1. Preheat air fryer to 400°F.
2. Place taquitos in a single layer in the air fryer basket.
3. Cook for 5-6 minutes or until they are heated through.

NOTES
Nutrition:

information is for taquitos only.

Air Fryers can vary by brand, check your taquitos early to make sure they don't overcook.

Do not overcrowd the air fryer.

Preheat the air fryer for best results.

Cook in batches if needed and add all taquitos to the air fryer to reheat before serving.

You can make your own homemade taquitos by rolling your favorite fillings in small tortillas. Be sure to oil the outside well.

Air Fryer Gnocchi And Squash With Brown Butter And Sage

Servings: 2

Ingredients:

- Deselect All
- Kosher salt
- 1 pound fresh or frozen gnocchi (see Cook's Note)
- 1 large delicata squash (about 1 1/2 pounds)
- Extra-virgin olive oil, for the squash and gnocchi
- Freshly ground black pepper
- 6 tablespoons unsalted butter
- 1/2 cup coarsely chopped walnuts
- 8 large fresh sage leaves, sliced into thin ribbons
- 1/2 cup coarsely grated or shaved Parmesan

Directions:

1. Special equipment: a 6-quart air fryer
2. Bring a large pot of salted water to a boil and line a baking sheet with paper towels.
3. Cook the gnocchi in the boiling water until they float, then remove them with a slotted spoon to the lined baking sheet to dry. Empty the pot, rinse and set aside.
4. Preheat a 6-quart air fryer to 375 degrees F.
5. Trim the ends of the squash, cut in half lengthwise and scoop out the seeds. Slice into roughly 1/4-inch-thick half-moons. Toss the squash in a medium bowl with 1 tablespoon olive oil, 1/2 teaspoon salt and several grinds of pepper.
6. Put the squash in the air fryer basket (reserve the bowl) and cook, flipping halfway through, until golden brown in spots, about 15 minutes. Transfer to a large serving bowl.
7. Preheat the air fryer again to 375 degrees F.
8. Add the gnocchi to the reserved bowl and toss with 2 teaspoons olive oil and 1/2 teaspoon salt. Transfer the gnocchi to the air fryer basket and cook, flipping halfway through, until golden and crispy, about 10 minutes. Transfer the gnocchi to the serving bowl with the squash.
9. While the gnocchi cooks, place the reserved pot over medium heat and melt the butter (make sure the pot is completely dry; any remaining water will make the butter splatter). Watching closely, cook the butter, swirling occasionally, until it begins to turn light golden and smell nutty, 2 to 3 minutes. Add the walnuts, sage and a pinch of salt and continue to cook, stirring; the butter will become foamy and begin to deepen in color. Continue to brown the butter until it is deep golden, about 2 more minutes. Pour the brown butter sage sauce over the gnocchi and squash, gently toss to coat and top with the Parmesan.
10. Cook's Note
11. If using shelf-stable gnocchi, increase the air fryer temperature to 400 degrees F and cook until golden and crispy, 13 to 15 minutes.

Low Country Boil Skewers

Ingredients:

- 6 baby red potatoes
- salt to taste
- 2 tbsp crab boil seasoning
- 1 ear of corn, shucked and cut into 1-inch rounds
- 4 tbsp butter
- 3 cloves garlic, finely chopped
- 2 tsp hot sauce
- 1 tsp cider vinegar
- 10 large shrimp, peeled and deveined
- 8 oz. smoked pork, sliced into ½ inch thick rounds
- lemon wedges, for serving

Directions:

1. Add the potatoes to a saucepan and cover with cold water. Add in salt to taste and 1 tablespoon of the seafood seasoning. Bring to a boil, reduce to a simmer and cook until the potatoes are tender, 10-12 minutes. Then, add in the corn in the last 5 minutes. Drain the water and let cool.
2. Melt the butter in a small skillet over medium heat. Once the butter is foaming, add the garlic and sauté until fragrant. Stir in the hot sauce and vinegar.

Then, remove from the heat and reserve half of the dressing.

3. Divide and thread the shrimp, sausage, potatoes and shrimp again onto your skewers. Brush half of the glaze onto the shrimp.

4. Using your Air Fryer Oven, place your skewers in the appliance and use the rotisserie setting. Air fry the skewers at 320°F for 10 minutes. Serve the skewers with lemon wedges and drizzle with the remaining sauce.

Air Fryer Fried Cheese Sticks

Servings: 6
Cooking Time: 20 Minutes

Ingredients:

- 12 part-skim mozzarella cheese sticks
- ¼ cup cornstarch
- 2 large eggs
- 2 cups italian seasoned breadcrumbs
- ¼ cup grated Parmesan cheese
- oil, for spraying
- marinara sauce, for dipping

Directions:

1. Separate mozzarella cheese sticks and freeze for 2 hours.

2. Place cornstarch in a large plastic bag. In a medium bowl, beat eggs. In a shallow dish or pie pan, combine breadcrumbs and Parmesan cheese. Place frozen cheese sticks in bag with cornstarch and shake. Remove one cheese stick and dip in beaten egg, shaking off any excess. Press into breadcrumb mixture and place on baking sheet lined with parchment paper. Repeat with remaining cheese sticks. Spray cheese sticks well with oil.

3. Working in batches of 6, place cheese sticks in air fryer basket. Do not overcrowd. Set temperature to 400 degrees. Air fry for 7 minutes, shaking basket frequently during cooking. Turn cheese sticks, and air fry for 3 minutes more. Repeat with remaining cheese sticks. Serve with warm marinara sauce on the side.

Air-fryer Jalapeño Poppers

Servings: 4

Ingredients:

- 2 ounces cream cheese, softened
- ¼ cup finely chopped cooked chicken breast (about 1 1/4 oz.)
- ¼ cup finely shredded sharp Cheddar cheese (1 oz.)
- ¼ cup finely chopped scallion
- 2 tablespoons hot sauce (such as Frank's RedHot)
- 2 teaspoons chopped fresh dill
- 4 large jalapeño peppers, halved lengthwise (about 1 1/2 oz. each)
- 2 tablespoons whole-wheat panko breadcrumbs
- Cooking spray

Directions:

1. Combine cream cheese, chicken, Cheddar, scallion, hot sauce and dill in a medium bowl; stir until well combined. Clean seeds and membranes from jalapeños and stuff evenly with the cream cheese mixture. Sprinkle with breadcrumbs. Place the stuffed jalapeños in the basket of an air fryer; coat with cooking spray. Cook at 370 degrees F until the tops are browned and the jalapeños are tender, about 10 minutes.

Air Fryer Pizzas

Servings: 2
Cooking Time: 10 Minutes

Ingredients:

- 1 8" pre-cooked Pizza Crust
- 1/4 cup (30 ml) Pizza Sauce or tomato sauce
- 3 Tablespoons (25 g) shredded Cheese
- salt , to taste
- black pepper , to taste
- OPTIONAL TOPPINGS
- Pepperoni, cooked Sausage, Bacon pieces, diced Ham, sliced or diced Tomatoes, Mushrooms, Pineapple, etc.
- OTHER SAUCE OPTIONS

- BBQ Sauce, Salsa, White (Alfredo) Sauce, Pesto, etc.
- EQUIPMENT
- Air Fryer
- Air Fryer Rack optional

Directions:

1. Place the pizza crust in air fryer bottom side up (make sure it is in just a single layer - cook in batches if needed for multiple pizzas).
2. Air Fry at 380°F/193°C about 3-5 minutes. Flip the crust over. Continue to Air fry at 380°F/193°C for another 3-5 minutes (if you want the crust extra crispy - air fry each side a couple minutes more).
3. Spread the sauce over the pizza crust. Top with cheese and add additional salt, pepper and other preferred toppings.
4. To keep your topping from flying around, place an air fryer rack over the pizza.
5. Air Fry the pizzas at 380°F/193°C for 2-4 minutes or until heated through and cheese is melted.
6. Remove from the air fryer and allow to cool for a minute or two before eating.

Air Fryer Mozzarella Sticks

Servings: 3-4
Cooking Time: 8 Minutes

Ingredients:

- 8 sticks mozzarella string cheese, cut in half
- ¼ cup all-purpose flour
- 2 large eggs, beaten
- ¾ cup bread crumbs
- 2 teaspoons olive oil
- 1 teaspoon Italian seasoning
- ½ teaspoon garlic powder
- ¼ teaspoon kosher salt
- Marinara sauce, for dipping

Directions:

1. Line a baking sheet with parchment paper. Set aside.
2. Place flour in a shallow bowl and set aside. In a second bowl, whisk egg until well beaten. In another shallow bowl, mix bread crumbs, vegetable oil, Italian seasoning, garlic powder, and salt and whisk to combine.
3. Dip each piece of mozzarella in the flour, then the egg, then roll in the breadcrumb mixture. Place the coated sticks on the baking sheet and freeze, uncovered, for at least 30 minutes, or until ready to fry.
4. Place the mozzarella sticks in the basket and spray them generously with cooking spray.
5. Air fry at 390 degrees F for 6-8 minutes (the cheese will begin to bubble), or until golden and crisp. Serve immediately with marinara sauce.

Air Fryer Pizza Sliders

Servings: 12
Cooking Time: 5 Minutes

Ingredients:

- 12 Slider rolls 4 English muffins can be substituted
- 1/2 cup pizza sauce
- 12 slices provolone cheese
- 1/2 cup mozzarella cheese
- 2 ounces pepperoni
- 1 teaspoon Italian seasoning

Directions:

1. Cover solid tray from toaster oven tightly with foil. Split Hawaiians nearly in half to make an open faced sandwich.
2. Spread pizza sauce on rolls. Add a layer of sliced cheese and then cover with additional shredded cheese if desired
3. Arrange pepperoni and other toppings on pizza sliders.
4. Sprinkle Italian seasong on top and bake for about 5 minutes at 350°F on the convection bake setting in an air fryer/toaster oven. Mini pizzas are ready when cheese is melted.°

NOTES

Substitutions are fine - pizza sauce is about the only ingredient I haven't substituted and enjoyed the result over the years

I enjoy pizza blend cheese with is a blend of white cheeses like mozzarella and provolone, but my son loves a cheddar blend

When available adding a layer of sliced provolone cheese will really step up the flavors of this dish

Toasting the bread or crust before topping with cheese and desired Ingredients:

Mushrooms, onions and peppers taste great as optional toppings

Pepperoni can be substituted for hard salami, cooked and crumbled sausage and bacon are delicious too

Cover baking tray tightly with foil for easier cleanup

Serve open-faced or make a sandwich, whichever is easier or more fun for you to eat

2 Ingredient Air Fryer Pizza

Servings: 2
Cooking Time: 10 Minutes

Ingredients:

- 240g (1 cup) natural or Greek yoghurt
- 350g (2 cups) self-raising flour
- grated cheese (enough to sprinkle on 2 small pizzas)
- pizza sauce/passata
- toppings of your choice (pepperoni, pineapple, peppers, chicken etc)

Directions:

1. Mix the self raising flour and yoghurt together (add more flour if necessary) until a dough consistency has been formed.
2. Split dough in
3. Roll each one out on a floured surface.
4. Place on a bit of parchment paper in air fryer basket and cook at 200C/400F for 8 to 10 minutes, turning over half way.
5. Take pizza out and add pizza sauce, grated cheese & any other toppings of your choice.
6. Return to air fryer basket and cook for a further 3 minutes.

7. Repeat with 2nd pizza.

Creamy Mac And Cheese

Ingredients:

- 250g boiled paste until al dente
- For the sauce:
- 5 tsp flour
- 60g butter
- 1 clove chopped garlic
- 1 tsp crushed green chilli
- Salt and pepper to taste
- 1/2 tsp onion powder
- 1/2 tsp mustard powder
- 1/2 tsp chilli flakes
- 2 cups milk
- 1 cup fresh cream
- 2 cups mozzarella
- 1 cup gouda or cheddar(your preference)for the top

Directions:

1. Make a roux with your butter and flour. Allow to cook so that you don't get a flour taste. Mix so that it doesn't burn. Cook for roughly 3 minutes.
2. Add milk and cream whisking continuously,you want to keep whisking so your sauce is lump free. Add in garlic, green chilli and other spices. Add in 1 cup mozzarella and whisk until cheese melts. Check seasoning and adjust accordingly.
3. Add your pasta to a dish that will fit in the air fryer, pour in half the sauce, mix and coat well. Add in the remaining cup of mozzarella and mix through. Pour over the remaining sauce and mix well. Top with cheddar/Gouda cheese.
4. Bake in your instantpot vortex air fryer on 160 degrees celsius for 10 minutes until cheese is melted.
5. Serve immediately. Garnish with chopped parsley

SNACKS & APPETIZERS RECIPES

Air Fryer Pasta Chips

Servings: 1
Cooking Time: 10 Minutes

Ingredients:
- 1 pound bowtie pasta
- 3 tablespoons olive oil
- 1/4 cup grated Parmesan cheese
- 1 teaspoon Italian seasoning
- 1 teaspoon garlic powder
- 1 teaspoon crushed red pepper

Directions:
1. Bring a large pot of salted water to a boil.
2. Add pasta and cook according to box directions until al dente.
3. Drain pasta and add to a large mixing bowl.
4. Add olive to pasta and toss.
5. Add in grated Parmesan cheese, Italian seasoning, garlic powder, and crushed red pepper.
6. Toss to combine.
7. Preheat air fryer to 400 degrees F.
8. Add pasta to preheated air fryer, covering the bottom of the basket and not overlapping in the basket.
9. Cook for 4 minutes on 400 degrees F.
10. Toss and cook for another 4-5 minutes at 400 degrees F. until you have reached your desired crispness.
11. Continue until all pasta chips have been made.
12. Serve with marinara sauce for dipping.

Air Fryer Green Beans

Servings: 4
Cooking Time: 6 Minutes

Ingredients:
- 1 lb green beans trimmed
- 2 tablespoons olive oil
- 1/2 teaspoon salt
- 1/2 teaspoon pepper

Directions:
1. Preheat the air fryer to 190C/375F.
2. In a mixing bowl, add the trimmed beans then toss through the olive oil, salt, and pepper.
3. Add a single layer of the beans to the air fryer basket and air fry for 8 minutes, shaking halfway through. Repeat the process until all the beans are cooked.
4. Sprinkle with parmesan cheese and add a squeeze of lemon juice.

NOTES

TO STORE: Leftovers can be stored in the refrigerator, covered, for up to 5 days.

TO FREEZE: Place the cooked and cooled beans in a ziplock bag and store them in the freezer for up to 6 months.

TO REHEAT: Either microwave for a few seconds or reheat in the air fryer for 1-2 minutes.

Air Fryer Frozen French Fries

Servings: 4
Cooking Time: 13 Minutes

Ingredients:

- 1 pound frozen french fries any style
- seasoned salt to taste

Directions:

1. Preheat air fryer to 400°F.
2. Add frozen fries to the air fryer, fill the basket about ½ full.
3. Cook 5 minutes and shake/toss the fries. Cook an additional 8-12 minutes or until crispy,Season with salt and serve immediately.

NOTES

Cook fries from frozen.

Preheat the air fryer for best results.

Do not overcrowd the air fryer.

Keep batches warm in the oven at 200°F and place all batches back into the air fryer for 1-2 minutes before serving.

Total Cook Time

Regular Frozen Fries: 12-14 minutes

Frozen Shoe String Fries: 7-9 minutes

Frozen Waffle Fries: 10-12 minutes

Frozen Sweet Potato Fries: 13-15 minutes

Air Fryer Sweet Potato Fries

Servings: 4
Cooking Time: 10 Minutes

Ingredients:

- 2 medium sweet potatoes washed and sliced
- 1 tablespoon olive oil
- 1/2 teaspoon salt
- 1/2 teaspoon pepper
- 1/2 teaspoon smoked paprika

Directions:

1. Wash and peel the sweet potatoes. Pat them dry then slice them into fries.
2. In a mixing bowl, add the potatoes and toss through the oil. Add the salt, pepper, and smoked paprika, and rub over the fries.
3. Place the sweet potato fries in the air fryer basket.
4. Air fry the potatoes at 200C/400F for 10 minutes, tossing halfway through.
5. Remove the potatoes from the air fryer and serve with dipping sauce.

NOTES

Serve fries with a sweet potato fry dipping sauce.

TO STORE: Leftovers can be stored in the refrigerator, covered, for up to three days.

TO FREEZE: Place the cooked and cooled fries in a ziplock bag and store them in the freezer for up to 6 months.

TO REHEAT: Either in a preheated oven or in the air fryer.

Air Fryer Sweet Potato Chips

Servings: 2
Cooking Time: 22 Minutes

Ingredients:

- 1 medium sweet potato
- 1 tablespoon canola oil
- 1 teaspoon kosher salt
- 3/4 teaspoon dried thyme leaves
- 1/2 teaspoon freshly ground black pepper
- 1/4 teaspoon paprika
- Pinch cayenne pepper (optional)
- Cooking spray

Directions:

1. Wash 1 sweet potato and dry well. Thinly slice 1/8-inch-thick with a knife or preferably on a mandoline. Place in a bowl, cover with cool water, and soak at room temperature for 20 minutes to remove the excess starch.
2. Drain the slices and pat very dry with towels. Place in a large bowl, add 1 tablespoon canola oil, 1 teaspoon kosher salt, 3/4 teaspoon dried thyme leaves, 1/2 teaspoon black pepper, 1/4 teaspoon

paprika, and a pinch cayenne pepper if using, and toss to combine.

3. Lightly coat Instant Vortex Plus 7-in-1 Air Fryer Oven rotisserie basket with cooking spray. Air fry in batches: place a single layer of sweet potato slices in the rotisserie basket. Place the rotisserie basket in the air fryer and press rotate. Preheat the air fryer to 360°F and set for 22 minutes. Air fry until the sweet potatoes are golden brown and the edges are crisp, 19 to 22 minutes.

4. Transfer the chips to a paper towel-lined plate to cool completely, they will crisp as they cool. Repeat with air frying the remaining sweet potato slices.

Air Fryer Potato Chips

Servings: 6
Cooking Time: 8 Minutes

Ingredients:

- 1 lb (453 g) Yukon gold potatoes
- 1 1/2 tbsp oil (see **NOTES**)
- 1/2 tsp garlic powder
- 1/2 tsp onion powder
- 3/4 tsp paprika powder
- Salt and pepper to taste (see **NOTES**)

Directions:

1. You can watch the short video for visual instructions.

2. Thinly slice the potatoes about 2-3 mm thick resp. 1/16th–1/8th inch (preferably with a mandoline) and soak them in water for about 20 minutes.

3. Then drain the water and pat-dry the potato slices with a kitchen towel.

4. Add them to a large bowl along with all other ingredients. Toss to combine.

5. Transfer a part of it to your air fryer (don't add too many, it's best to cook them in batches) and air-fry for about 8-15 minutes at 350 F (175 C). The time really depends on the thickness of the potatoes. Mine were super thin (about 2 mm), so it took just 8 minutes.

6. Check the recipe **NOTES** below for the oven- and microwave methods.

7. Enjoy with ketchup, vegan mayo, yum yum sauce, or a dip of choice.

NOTES

Oven method: Bake them in the oven on a lined baking sheet (single layer) at 375 F (190 C) for about 30 minutes (or until golden), flipping after 20 minutes.

Microwave method: Slice a piece of parchment paper to fit your microwave (or use a small silicone mat). Spread the potato chips in a thin layer over the parchment paper. Microwave at high power for 2 minutes, flip, and microwave for a further 1 1/2 - 2 minutes. Depending on the thickness of your slices, you may need to continue cooking them longer. To do so, reduce the heat to 50% and cook in 30-second increments until crispy and golden. The time will vary based on the power of your microwave and the thickness of the potato slices, so keep an eye on them.

Oil-free: I tried the microwave method without oil, and it worked incredibly well.

Cooking time is per batch and total time doesn't include soaking time.

Sodium was calculated with 1/2 tsp of salt in total. Feel free to use less or more to taste.

Crispy Kale Chips

Servings: 4
Cooking Time: 15 Minutes

Ingredients:

- 250g kale, destalked and chopped
- 2 tsp olive oil
- 1/2 tsp dried dill
- 1/2 tsp garlic powder
- 1/2 tsp onion powder
- 1 pinch black pepper (to taste)

Directions:

1. Place the kale in a bowl and drizzle over the oil. Massage the oil into the leaves with your hands.

2. Heat the air fryer to 180°C and add the kale leaves to the basket in a single layer, working in batches. Cook for 3-4 minutes until crisp, shaking once or twice and watching carefully for any overcooked leaves. Repeat with the remaining kale.
3. Whisk the seasoning ingredients together in a small bowl and sprinkle over the crispy kale chips before serving.

Air Fryer Chickpeas

Servings: 4
Cooking Time: 13 Minutes

Ingredients:

- 1 can chickpeas 15-16 ounces, drained
- 1 tablespoon olive oil
- 1 teaspooon ranch seasoning or seasoning of choice
- Homemade Ranch Seasoning
- 1 tablespoon dried parsley
- 1 teaspoon dried dill
- 2 teaspoons garlic powder
- 1 teaspoon onion powder
- 1/2 teaspoon salt
- 1/2 teaspoon ground black pepper

Directions:

1. Pour the can of chickpeas into a strainer, then drain chickpeas and rinse them well under cold water. Pat chickpeas dry with a clean kitchen towel or paper towels.
2. Place chickpeas in a medium bowl with oil and toss them until they are well coated. Add in your choice of seasonings and toss them together fully coating the chickpeas.
3. Pour chickpeas into the air fryer basket in a single layer, leaving space between chickpeas so they cook evenly.
4. Air fry at 400 degrees F for 13-15 minutes, until they are crispy and a light golden brown.
5. Serve seasoned chickpeas at any temperature.
6. Homemade Ranch Seasoning

7. In a small bowl combine dried parsley, dried dill, garlic powder, onion powder, salt and ground black pepper and crush them together (this releases the oils in spices for maximum flavor).

NOTES

Optional Seasonings: Salt (½ teaspoon), Indian spice blend, everything but the bagel seasoning, ground cumin, Italian seasoning, BBQ seasoning, chaat masala, curry powder, chili powder, Korean chili flakes, garlic powder, elote seasoning,

Optional Favorite Garnishes: A bit of lemon zest, tablespoon lemon juice or lime juice for some acidity. Roasted garlic with fresh herbs like a teaspoon dill, teaspoon chives or a teaspoon parsley for freshness. Freshly grated parmesan or pecorino Romano cheese.

Cooking Tips: If you are cooking batches of chickpeas place them on a baking sheet so they can completely cool and remain crispy. When shopping know that chickpeas and garbanzo beans are the same exact thing, they just have two different names.

Air Fryer Ravioli

Servings: 2
Cooking Time: 6 Minutes

Ingredients:

- 12 frozen ravioli
- 1/2 cup buttermilk*
- 1/2 cup Italian breadcrumbs
- ALSO
- Marinara sauce for dipping
- Oil for spritzing

Directions:

1. Preheat air fryer to 400 degrees.
2. Place two bowls side by side. Put the buttermilk in one and breadcrumbs in the other.
3. Dip each piece of ravioli into the buttermilk then breadcrumbs, making sure to coat it as best as possible.

4. Place each breaded ravioli into the air fryer in one single layer and cook for 6-7 minutes, spritzing the tops with oil halfway through.
5. Remove the air fryer and enjoy immediately with marinara or freeze for up to 3 months.

NOTES

*substitute buttermilk by filling a large measuring cup with 2 teaspoons of vinegar and filling it up to the 1/2 cup line. Stir, then wait 5 minutes. Now you have buttermilk!

How to Cook Frozen Fried Ravioli in the Air Fryer:

Cook ravioli in a preheated air fryer at 350 degrees for 3-4 minutes, spritzing with oil before cooking.

Air Fryer Butternut Squash Recipe

Servings: 4-6
Cooking Time: 24-32 Minutes

Ingredients:

- 2 pounds butternut squash (1 small)
- 1 1/2 tablespoons olive oil
- 1 teaspoon kosher salt
- 1/2 teaspoon garlic powder
- 1/4 teaspoon freshly ground black pepper
- SAVORY VARIATION (OPTIONAL):
- 2 teaspoons ground cumin
- 1 teaspoon paprika
- SWEET VARIATION (OPTIONAL):
- 2 tablespoons maple syrup
- 2 teaspoons ground cinnamon

Directions:

1. Heat an air fryer to 400°F. Meanwhile, if needed, peel 1 small butternut squash, halve and remove the seeds, and cut the flesh into 1/2-inch cubes (about 5 cups). Transfer the squash to a large bowl.
2. Add 1 1/2 tablespoons olive oil, 1 teaspoon kosher salt, 1/2 teaspoon garlic powder, and 1/4 teaspoon black pepper to the squash. If making the savory variation, also add 2 teaspoons ground cumin and 1

teaspoon paprika. If making the sweet variation, also add 2 tablespoons maple syrup and 2 teaspoons ground cinnamon. Toss to coat.
3. Working in batches, add the butternut squash to the air fryer basket in a single layer. Air fry until the butternut squash is tender with browned and crispy edges, shaking the basket or tossing halfway through, 12 to 16 minutes total.
4. Transfer to a bowl and loosely tent with aluminum foil to keep warm while you air fry the remaining squash.

NOTES

Make ahead: The butternut squash can be cut up to 3 days in advance and refrigerated in an airtight container.

Storage: Leftovers can be refrigerated in an airtight container for up to 4 days.

Air Fryer Onion Rings

Servings: 4-6
Cooking Time: 10 Minutes

Ingredients:

- 1 large sweet (Vidalia) onion, sliced into ½-inch rings
- 2 large eggs
- ⅔ cup buttermilk
- ⅔ cup all-purpose flour
- ½ teaspoon kosher salt
- ½ teaspoon black pepper
- ½ teaspoon garlic powder
- 1 ½ cups panko bread crumbs

Directions:

1. Peel onion and cut it into ½-inch thick slices. Separate the slices and place them on a plate. Set aside.
2. In a wide, shallow bowl, lightly beat the eggs with the buttermilk until well combined. In a second bowl, combine the flour, salt, pepper, and garlic powder. Place the panko bread crumbs in a third bowl.

3. Dip each onion ring into the flour, then the buttermilk mixture, and then dredge it through the bread crumbs, pressing to adhere. Set aside on a baking sheet and repeat with remaining rings. Spray the rings with an EVO Oil sprayer.

4. Preheat the air fryer to 380 degrees F.

5. Transfer the rings into the air fryer basket in a single layer, nesting the smaller ones inside the larger ones but leaving a little space between each ring. Don't overcrowd the basket, and work in batches if necessary.

6. Air fry for 9-12 minutes, or until golden brown and crispy.

7. Sprinkle with salt if desired, and serve.

NOTES

HOW TO REHEAT ONION RINGS IN THE AIR FRYER:

Preheat your air fryer to 350 degrees.

Place the leftover onion rings in the air fryer and cook for 2 to 3 minutes until warmed thoroughly and crispy.

Air Fryer Frozen Onion Rings

Servings: 2
Cooking Time: 12 Minutes

Ingredients:

- 6 ounces (170 g) Frozen Onion Rings
- salt , to taste
- black pepper , to taste
- EQUIPMENT
- Air Fryer

Directions:

1. Place the frozen onion rings in the air fryer basket and spread out evenly. No oil spray is needed.

2. Air Fry at 400°F/205°C for 10 minutes. Shake and gently stir about halfway through cooking. If cooking larger batches, or if the onion rings don't cook evenly, try turning them multiple times on following batches.

3. If needed air fry at 400°F/205°C for an additional 1-4 minutes or until crisped to your liking. Season with salt & pepper, if desired.

NOTES

Air Frying Tips and **NOTES**:

No Oil Necessary. Cook Frozen - Do not thaw first.

Shake or turn if needed. Don't overcrowd the air fryer basket.

Recipe timing is based on a non-preheated air fryer. If cooking in multiple batches of onion rings back to back, the following batches may cook a little quicker.

Recipes were tested in 3.7 to 6 qt. air fryers. If using a larger air fryer, the onion rings might cook quicker so adjust cooking time.

Remember to set a timer to shake/flip/toss as directed in recipe.

Air Fried Acorn Squash

Servings: 4
Cooking Time: 20 Minutes

Ingredients:

- 1 acorn squash
- 1/4 cup (45 g) butter , melted
- 1 Tablespoon (10 g) brown sugar , or more to taste
- 1/2 teaspoon (2.5 g) kosher salt , or to taste
- Black pepper , to taste
- OPTIONAL TOPPINGS:
- melted butter
- chopped roasted nuts
- pomegranate seeds
- EQUIPMENT
- Air Fryer

Directions:

1. Trim the top & bottom off the acorn squash, and then cut the squash in half from top to bottom. Scoop out the seeds using a spoon. Lay the squash cut side down on the cutting board, and cut the squash into half rings, about 1/2-inch thick.

2. In a small bowl, combine the melted butter, brown sugar, salt and pepper. Toss the acorn squash rings

in the butter mixture until well coated. Place in the air fryer basket.

3. Air Fry at 375°F for about 15-20 minutes or until tender, flipping the squash after the first 10 minutes. Remember to flip so the squash cooks evenly.

4. You can make it extra delicious by drizzling the squash with extra melted butter, chopped nuts, and pomegranate seeds. Taste for seasoning and add a little more salt & pepper if desired.

Air Fryer Kale Chips

Servings: 4
Cooking Time: 5 Minutes

Ingredients:

- 1 bunch kale (lacinato kale preferred, but any kind will do), stemmed, washed, and patted dry
- 2 tbsp. extra-virgin olive oil
- 1 tbsp. fresh lemon juice
- 1/2 c. finely grated Parmesan
- Kosher salt
- Freshly ground black pepper
- Optional seasonings: everything bagel seasoning, smoked paprika, crushed red pepper flakes, or garlic powder

Directions:

1. Tear kale leaves into large chip-sized pieces and transfer to a medium bowl. Drizzle with oil and lemon juice and toss to combine. Using your fingers, ensure each piece is lightly and evenly coated.

2. Add Parmesan and toss to combine; season with salt and black pepper, then add any optional seasonings to taste. Toss again to combine.

3. In an air-fryer basket, arrange kale in a single layer. Cook at 350° until edges are just starting to brown, 3 to 5 minutes. (The more delicate the kale variety, the quicker it will cook.) Transfer kale to a sheet pan and let cool in a single layer. Kale will continue to crisp as it cools.

Sloppy Joe Fries

Ingredients:

- 1 large onion
- Garlic
- 1 tbsp tomato puree
- 1 lb. ground beef
- 1 tbsp thyme
- 1 tbsp oregano
- 1 tsp pepper
- 1 tsp salt

Directions:

1. Toppings:
2. Chop 1 large onion
3. Using a stovetop or pressure cooker, roast garlic topped with olive oil at 350 F
4. Smash roasted garlic into paste
5. For this recipe we used one of our pressure cookers. At this step, saute onions using olive oil.
6. After the onions have cooked a little, add the mashed garlic, tomato puree, and ground beef.
7. After meat is browned, add 1 cup of canned tomatoes and spices.
8. Set aside. Time to make the fries!
9. Fries:
10. Peel 3 russet potatoes and chop into skinny wedges
11. Coat french fries with some olive oil and salt and pepper.
12. Add coated potatoes into air fryer.
13. Cook at 400 F for 8 minutes
14. After the 8 minutes take the basket out and shake fries carefully.
15. Cook for 8 minutes at 400 F
16. Place toppings on fries and cheese (optional)
17. Enjoy

Trader Joes Frozen Handsome Cut Potato Fries In The Air Fryer

Servings: 8
Cooking Time: 17 Minutes

Ingredients:

- 24 oz. (425 g) Trader Joes Frozen Handsome Cut Potato Fries
- Kosher salt or sea salt , to taste
- ground black pepper , to taste (optional)
- EQUIPMENT
- Air Fryer

Directions:

1. Place the frozen fries in air fryer basket and spread them evenly over the basket. If you have a large air fryer, you can cook a whole bag at a time. Otherwise just cook a half a bag per batch for best results. A single layer is best and two layers deep is about the max you should do. You don't need thaw them first or to spray any extra oil.

2. Air fry the frozen fries at 400°F/205°C for about 12-17 minutes. About halfway through cooking, shake the basket and gently turn the fries. Try not to break them. For crisper, evenly cooked fries, turn them multiples times while cooking.

3. If needed, Air Fry for additional 1-3 minutes to crisp to your preferred liking. Season with salt and pepper if desired.

NOTES

No Oil Necessary. Cook Fries Frozen - Do not thaw first. Shake several times for even cooking & Don't overcrowd fryer basket.

If cooking in multiple batches, the first batch will take longer to cook if Air Fryer is not already pre-heated.

Recipes were cooked in 3-4 qt air fryers. If using a larger air fryer, the recipe might cook quicker so adjust cooking time.

Remember to set a timer to shake/flip/toss the food as directed in recipe.

Air Fryer Pumpkin Seeds

Servings: 4
Cooking Time: 12 Minutes

Ingredients:

- 1 cup pumpkin seeds
- 1 Tablespoon olive oil
- 1/2 teaspoon kosher salt
- 1/2 teaspoon cinnamon
- 1 Tablespoon brown sugar

Directions:

1. Carefully remove the pulp from the pumpkin and separate the pumpkin seeds from the pulp. Boil the seeds for a few moments in a pot of boiling water to help remove the pulp. You may need to run the seeds and any pulp through running water in a colander to help remove any remaining pumpkin flesh after boiling.

2. Once the seeds have been cleaned, place the clean pumpkin seeds on a paper towel and allow them to dry.

3. Preheat the Air Fryer to 370 degrees Fahrenheit. Prepare the air fryer basket with nonstick cooking spray if needed.

4. Place the fresh pumpkin seeds in a large bowl and coat with olive oil. Once the seeds have been coated in oil, add the kosher salt and brown sugar. Toss until the seeds are fully coated.

5. Place the prepared pumpkin seeds in a single layer in the prepared air fryer basket.

6. Cook on 320 degrees Fahrenheit for 10-12 minutes, tossing the seeds halfway through cook time. Add an additional minute or two for more crispy homemade pumpkin seeds.

NOTES

What seasonings can I use for airfryer roasted pumpkin seeds?

You can easily change the flavors of roasted pumpkin seeds. Try seasoning the seeds with different spices such as garlic salt, garlic powder, black pepper, pumpkin pie spice, or even add a little batch of cajun creole seasoning. There are tons of options for this great snack.

How do I store roasted pumpkin seeds?

Roasted pumpkin seeds will stay fresh for a couple of days at room temperature when stored in an airtight container. Store roasted pumpkin seeds in an airtight container in the refrigerator for up to a week.

Loaded Cheese Fries

Servings: 6
Cooking Time: 30 Minutes

Ingredients:

- Fries
- 32 ounces frozen french fries or 8 cups homemade french fries
- Toppings
- 1 ½ cups cheddar cheese
- 3 tablespoons bacon cooked and crumbled, or real bacon bits
- 1 cup brown gravy homemade or packet, optional
- ½ cup sour cream
- 2 green onions thinly sliced

Directions:

1. Preheat the oven to 425°F (or cook fries in the air fryer per directions in the **NOTES**).
2. Add the fries to a rimmed baking sheet and cook for 25-30 minutes or until extra crisp, stirring after 15 minutes.
3. Once the fries are crisp, remove them from the oven and turn the broiler on to 500°F.
4. Top the fries with cheddar and bacon and place back into the oven for 1-3 minutes or until the cheese is melted.
5. Top with green onions. If using, drizzle with brown gravy and top with sour cream. Serve immediately.

NOTES

Thicker fries may need more time, thinner fries may need a bit less time. Appliances can vary but it is easy to check on the fries a couple of minutes early and add more time if needed.

To make frozen fries in the air fryer, cook several smaller batches. Once ready to serve, add all fries to the air fryer basket and cook at 390°F for 10-14 minutes or until crisp. Top with cheese and bacon. Cook in the air fryer for an additional 2-3 minutes.

Spicy Halloumi Fries With Chilli Butter Sweetcorn Cobettes

Servings: 4

Ingredients:

- 2 blocks of halloumi (225g each)
- 75g plain flour
- 1 tsp sumac
- 1 tsp za'atar
- 1 lemon
- 150g natural Greek yogurt
- 2 tbsp coriander, chopped
- Cooking spray or oil
- For the chilli corn butter
- 50g butter, softened
- 2 tsp tomato ketchup
- 1 tsp honey
- 1/2 tsp rose harissa
- 4 sweetcorn cobettes
- COOKING MODE
- When entering cooking mode - We will enable your screen to stay 'always on' to avoid any unnecessary interruptions whilst you cook!

Directions:

1. Drain halloumi and pat dry. Cut into thick fries.
2. In a bowl, mix the flour and sumac, za'atar. Dip halloumi into the flour to lightly coat.
3. Insert crisper plates into both drawers. Liberally spray drawer 1 with cooking spray or oil, add halloumi and spray with oil. Insert drawer into unit.
4. Make chilli butter: In a bowl, place butter, tomato ketchup, honey and harissa, beat together till smooth. Using a pastry brush, or back of a teaspoon,

brush each cobettes with butter. Reserve remaining butter by placing in cling film, form into a sausage shape, wrap and chill whilst corn is cooking. Place corn onto crisper plate in zone 2 drawer. Insert drawer into unit.

5. Select zone 1, select AIR FRY, set temperature to 200°C and time for 18 minutes. Select zone 2, select ROAST, set temperature to 180°C and time to 15 minutes. Select SYNC. START/STOP to begin.

6. When zone 1 reaches 10 minutes, rearrange halloumi fries and sweetcorn. Repeat when zone 1 reaches 6 minutes

7. Cut chilli butter into 4 and place on top of corn. Serve with halloumi topped with Greek yogurt swirled with chopped coriander

Air Fryer Green Bean Fries

Servings: 3-4
Cooking Time: 5 Minutes

Ingredients:
- 6 oz fresh raw green beans
- 1 egg
- 1 egg white
- ½ cup panko crumbs, divided
- 2 tablespoons grated parmesan
- ½ tablespoon garlic powder
- 1 teaspoon paprika
- ¼ teaspoon salt
- ⅛ teaspoon ground black pepper

Directions:
1. Preheat your air fryer to 400 degrees F and wash and trim your green beans.

2. Whisk your egg and egg white in a medium bowl.

3. In a small bowl, use the back of a large spoon and crush ¼ cup of panko crumbs as fine as you can. These smaller crumbs will help coat all of your green beans. In a wide dish, combine the crushed panko and the remaining ¼ cup of panko crumbs, parmesan, and seasoning.

4. Place a few green beans in the egg wash, making sure to coat it well. Use a fork to lift them out, shaking any excess egg off. Place it in the panko and use your fingers to cover the green bean, flipping it over on all sides to get as much covered as possible.

5. Lay your breaded green beans in the basket. Leave room around them to allow them to get nice and crispy. Place them in the air fryer and set the temperature to 400 degrees. Cook for 4 to 5 minutes and then check them.

6. Serve green bean fries on their own or with your favorite dipping sauce.

NOTES
HOW TO REHEAT FRIED GREEN BEANS IN THE AIR FRYER
Lay leftover green bean fries in the air fryer in a single layer.
Cook at 400 degrees F for 3 minutes.

BREAKFAST & BRUNCH RECIPES

Air Fryer Scrambled Eggs

Servings: 2
Cooking Time: 12 Minutes

Ingredients:

- 4 eggs large
- 1/2 teaspoon salt
- 1/2 teaspoon ground black pepper
- 1/2 teaspoon avocado spray or non stick cooking spray
- optional shredded cheese

Directions:

1. Preheat the air fryer to 350 degrees Fahrenheit.
2. Add the eggs to a medium sized bowl with the salt and pepper and whisk for 60 seconds, or until fully combined. (If adding cheese to the eggs, do so during this step.) Prepare the dish with butter or avocado spray to prevent sticking.
3. Add the whisked eggs to the bowl and place the bowl into the basket of the air fryer.
4. Air fry the eggs at 350 degrees Fahrenheit for 10-12 minutes, stirring the eggs with a fork every 3-4 minutes.
5. Carefully remove the dish from the air fryer basket and serve on a plate with your favorite breakfast items.

NOTES

This recipe was made in a 5.8 qt basket style Cosori air fryer. If you are using a different brand of air fryer, you may need to adjust the cooking time slightly.

Eggs are really quite fun to play around with and add different tastes and flavors. I'm always amazed at how I can cook up a batch of eggs and make every serving taste unique.

Add fresh herbs - The easiest way to make eggs taste super fresh is to add some fresh herbs to them. (This is especially fun if you grow your own herbs from your garden!) Fresh cilantro is one of my favorite toppings for eggs and it adds a nice pop of color, too.

Make spicy eggs - Do you love extra heat? I hear ya - I do, too! Add some hot sauce to your serving size to make this easy recipe a spicy one. Just be sure that you're adding the heat to your own bowl so that it doesn't make the entire dish hot!

Cheese please - Adding some cheese to the top portion of the eggs is always a good idea. I love eggs and cheddar cheese!

Air Fryer Frozen Garlic Bread

Servings: 4
Cooking Time: 9 Minutes

Ingredients:

- 4 Frozen Garlic Bread (without cheese or with)
- fresh chopped parsley , optional
- EQUIPMENT
- Air Fryer

Directions:

1. Place the frozen garlic bread in the air fryer basket and spread in an even layer (make sure they aren't overlapping). No oil spray is needed.
2. Air Fry at 340°F/170°C for 5 minutes. If the garlic bread is without cheese, flip the garlic bread over. If it has cheese, don't flip or else you'll lose your cheese.
3. Continue to Air Fry at 340°F/170°C for another 1-5 minutes or until cooked to your desired golden crispness. If you're cooking only 1-2 pieces of garlic bread it might take about 5-6 minutes total time, depending on how crisp you like your toast. Test a piece first and you'll know more of what your preferred timing is like. Top with optional chopped parsley if desired.

NOTES

Air Frying Tips and **NOTES**:

No Oil Necessary. Cook Frozen - Do not thaw first.

Cook in a single layer in the air fryer basket.

Recipe timing is based on a non-preheated air fryer. If cooking in multiple batches back to back, the following batches may cook a little quicker.

Recipes were tested in 3.7 to 6 qt. air fryers. If using a larger air fryer, they might cook quicker so adjust cooking time.

Bacon Spinach Breakfast Casserole With Gruyère

Servings: 8
Cooking Time: 45 Minutes

Ingredients:

- Cooking spray
- 8 slices center-cut bacon (chopped)
- ½ cup finely diced shallots
- 5-ounce package baby spinach
- 8 ounces shredded Gruyère cheese (2 cups total (I like Finlandia))
- 12 large eggs
- 1 cup nonfat milk
- ½ teaspoon kosher salt
- Freshly ground black pepper (to taste)

Directions:

1. Preheat oven to 350 degrees F. Spray a 9" x 13" casserole dish with cooking spray and set aside.
2. In a large skillet, cook the bacon over medium heat until cooked through. Using a slotted spoon, transfer the bacon to a paper towel lined plate.
3. Remove and discard all but 2 tablespoons of the bacon grease then add the shallots.
4. Sauté the shallots until fragrant and they start to brown on the edges, about 2 minutes.
5. Add half the spinach and toss to mix with the shallots then add the rest and toss again.
6. Cook, stirring and tossing for about 3 minutes, until spinach is wilted. Remove the pan from heat and set aside.

7. In a large bowl, whisk the eggs.
8. Set aside 1 cup of the cheese then add the remainder to the eggs. Add the milk, salt, pepper, cooked spinach mixture and bacon then mix to thoroughly combine.
9. Pour egg mixture into the prepared dish then sprinkle remaining cheese evenly over the top.
10. Bake for 35 minutes, then move the oven rack to the second slot closest to the top, switch the oven to broil and cook an additional 2-3 minutes, until browned, watching closely to make sure it doesn't burn.
11. Allow to cool for 10 minutes then cut into 8 pieces and serve immediately.

Pull Apart Cheese Bread

Ingredients:

- Loaf crusty rustic bread
- 1 stick of unsalted butter, melted
- 1 bunch green onions, minced
- 2 Tbsp. parsley, minced
- 1 Tbsp. onion powder
- 1 Tbsp. garlic powder
- 1/2 cup mozzarella cheese, shredded
- 1/2 cup cheddar cheese, shredded

Directions:

1. Cut the bread loaf in a 1-inch grid pattern, making sure not to slice all the way through.
2. In a bowl, combine the melted butter, green onions, parsley, garlic powder and onion powder.
3. Using a pastry brush, brush the butter mixture all over the bread, getting into all of the cracks.
4. Sprinkle the top with cheese and making sure to get into the cracks of the bread.
5. Insert loaf into the air fryer and bake at 350F for about 5 minutes. Serve immediately!

Easy Air Fryer Omelette

Ingredients:

- 2 eggs
- 1/4 cup milk
- Pinch of salt
- Fresh meat and veggies, diced (I used red bell pepper, green onions, ham and mushrooms)
- 1 teaspoon McCormick Good Morning Breakfast Seasoning – Garden Herb
- 1/4 cup shredded cheese (I used cheddar and mozzarella)
- Cook Mode Prevent your screen from going dark

Directions:

1. In a small bowl, mix the eggs and milk until well combined.
2. Add a pinch of salt to the egg mixture.
3. Add your veggies to the egg mixture.
4. Pour the egg mixture into a well-greased 6″x3″ pan.
5. Place the pan into the basket of the air fryer.
6. Cook at 350° Fahrenheit for 8-10 minutes.
7. Halfway through cooking sprinkle the breakfast seasoning onto the eggs and sprinkle the cheese over the top.
8. Use a thin spatula to loosen the omelette from the sides of the pan and transfer to a plate.
9. Garnish with extra green onions, optional

Air Fryer Cheese & Ham Croissant

Ingredients:

- Croissant
- Ham
- Mayonnaise
- Cheese of choice

Directions:

1. Cut the croissant in half
2. Butter the croissant using butter or mayonnaise
3. Layer the ham, followed by cheese.
4. On top butter again with mayonnaise and sprinkle with cheese on top.
5. Air Fry for 3 minutes at 170C and cheesy cheesy, enjoy!

Air Fryer Frozen Toaster Scramble

Servings: 1
Cooking Time: 8 Minutes

Ingredients:

- 1 Frozen Toaster Scramble
- EQUIPMENT
- Air Fryer

Directions:

1. Remove frozen toaster scrambles from package and take out of plastic wrap.
2. Place the frozen toaster scramble in the air fryer basket. If cooking multiple toaster scrambles, spread out into a single even layer. Don't overlay or else the won't cook evenly. No oil spray is needed.
3. Air Fry at 340°F/171°C for 6 minutes. Flip the toaster scramble over.
4. Continue to Air Fry at 340°F/171°C for another 1-2 minutes, or until golden and filling is heated through.

NOTES

Air Frying Tips and **NOTES**:

No Oil Necessary. Cook Frozen - Do not thaw first.

Remember to turn/flip after the first 6 minutes. Don't overcrowd the air fryer basket.

Recipe timing is based on a non-preheated air fryer. If cooking in multiple batches of hot pockets back to back, the following batches may cook a little quicker.

Recipes were tested in 3.7 to 6 qt. air fryers. If using a larger air fryer, the toaster scrambles might cook quicker so adjust cooking time.

Air Fryer Coconut Macaroons

Servings: 1

Ingredients:

- 2 large egg whites
- 4 tsp. honey
- Pinch of kosher salt
- 1 1/2 c. unsweetened shredded coconut
- Olive oil cooking spray
- 1/2 c. semisweet chocolate chips
- 1 tsp. virgin coconut oil

Directions:

1. In a medium bowl, whisk egg whites, honey, and salt until foamy. Add coconut and stir to combine.
2. Line an air-fryer basket with foil, leaving about a 1" overhang on 2 opposite sides. Lightly coat foil with cooking spray.
3. Tightly pack coconut mixture into a tablespoon measuring spoon. Carefully arrange mounds flat side down in prepared basket, spacing about 1/4" apart. Cook at 320° until set on top and light golden in places, 3 to 5 minutes. Flip and continue to cook until flat side is set and dry to the touch, 1 to 2 minutes more. Using foil overhang, carefully remove macaroons from air fryer. Let cool.
4. Line a small baking sheet or plate with parchment. In a small heatproof bowl, combine chips and oil. Microwave on high, stirring, until just melted and smooth, about 1 minute.
5. Dip flat side of macaroons into chocolate mixture. Transfer to prepared sheet chocolate side down. Refrigerate until chocolate is set, about 20 minutes.
6. Make Ahead: Macaroons can be made 1 week ahead. Store in an airtight container in refrigerator.

Coronation Scotch Quails Eggs

Servings: 4

Ingredients:

- 12 quail eggs
- Iced water
- 300g good-quality pork sausage meat
- 2 tbsp fresh parsley, chopped
- 1 tsp Worcestershire sauce
- 1 tbsp onion chutney
- Salt and freshly ground black pepper
- 1 medium egg, beaten
- 50g plain flour
- 75g dried breadcrumbs
- COOKING MODE
- When entering cooking mode - We will enable your screen to stay 'always on' to avoid any unnecessary interruptions whilst you cook!

Directions:

1. Insert crisper plate into Zone 1 drawer. Place 12 whole eggs on top of crisper plate and insert drawer into unit. Select Zone 1, turn the dial to select AIR FRY, set temperature to 150°C, and set time to 5-6 minutes, depending how you want eggs cooked, soft or hard. Press the dial to begin cooking. When cooking is complete remove eggs with silicone tongs and plunge into iced water to stop eggs cooking further. Allow to cool, then peel shells off eggs and reserve.
2. In a large bowl, add the sausage meat, parsley, Worcestershire sauce and onion chutney together with plenty of seasoning and stir everything together until evenly mixed. Divide mixture into 4 balls and place between cling film. Squash one of the balls until it's as flat as possible in the cling film. Tip the flour onto a plate and season well. One at a time, lightly flour each cooked egg, then use the cling film to help roll the sausage meat around the egg to completely encase. Repeat with the remaining sausage balls and eggs.

3. Crack egg into a shallow bowl and beat with a fork. Add the breadcrumbs onto another plate.

4. Roll coated eggs in flour again, roll coated eggs in beaten egg and finally roll in breadcrumbs. Chill for 30 minutes.

5. Place eggs back in Zone 1 drawer. Spray eggs with oil. Turn the dial to select AIR FRY, set temperature to 180°C, and set time to 8-9 minutes. Press the dial to begin cooking.

6. Serve hot or cold.

Air-fryer Quesadillas

Servings: 6

Ingredients:
- 1-1/2 cups shredded Mexican cheese blend
- 1/2 cup salsa
- 4 flour tortillas (8 inches), warmed
- Cooking spray

Directions:
1. Preheat air fryer to 375°. Combine cheese and salsa; spread over half of each tortilla. Fold tortilla over. In batches, place tortillas in a single layer on a greased tray in air-fryer basket; spritz with cooking spray. Cook until golden brown and cheese has melted, 5-7 minutes. Cut into wedges.

Air Fried Cadbury Eggs

Servings: 4
Cooking Time: 6 Minutes

Ingredients:
- 1 can Pillsbury Crescents 8 ounces
- 4 Cadbury Crème Eggs

Directions:
1. To make these fried Cadbury eggs, begin by unwrapping each egg from their foil wrapper.

2. Open the crescent rolls and separate dough into the pre-cut triangles. Wrap one egg in each piece of pastry, making sure to completely cover the egg. Pinch the dough to cover any exposed chocolate.

3. To prepare the air fryer basket, lightly spray or line with parchment paper, to prevent sticking. Place each wrapped egg in the air fryer basket. If making multiple eggs, keep them in a single layer.

4. Air Fry at 350° Fahrenheit for 6 minutes, until they are golden brown.

5. Serve warm, or you can allow the eggs to cool so the liquid crème filling can become less gooey.

NOTES

I use the Cosori 5.8 basket air fryer and 6 minutes was perfect. I did not preheat air fryer. Because all air fryers are not the same, you may need to add another minute cook time.

Air Fryer Egg Bites

Servings: 4
Cooking Time: 6 Minutes

Ingredients:
- 6 eggs
- ¼ cup mozzarella cheese shredded
- ¼ cup ham diced
- ¼ cup vegetables diced (peppers, onion, mushrooms)
- salt & pepper to taste
- 2 teaspoons parsley

Directions:
1. Preheat your air fryer to 350°F.
2. Spray the silicone egg mold with the cooking spray.
3. Whisk the eggs in a measuring cup and stir in the remaining ingredients.
4. Pour the egg mixture into the silicone molds until they are about 90% full.
5. Put them in the air fryer and cook for 11-13 minutes. Remove from the air fryer and stir the mixture after 7 minutes and continue cooking.
6. Test with a toothpick if it comes out clean they are done, if not cook for another 1-2 minutes.

Air Fryer Hard Boiled Eggs

Servings: 4-6

Ingredients:

- 4 large eggs
- Water and ice, for ice bath

Directions:

1. Preheat air fryer to 270°. Add eggs and cook for 15 minutes for hard boiled eggs. For eggs with jammier yolks, cook for 12 to 13 minutes; for soft boiled eggs, 9 to 10 minutes.
2. While the eggs cook, prepare an ice bath. As soon as the eggs are done, transfer them to the ice bath to halt the cooking. Once cooled, peel the eggs and serve.

Breakfast Bombs

Servings: 4-6

Ingredients:

- 1 tube refrigerated biscuit dough
- 1 tbsp. butter
- 4 eggs
- 2 tbsp. whole milk
- 1 tbsp. finely chopped chives
- 4 slices bacon, cooked and crumbled
- 3/4 c. shredded cheddar
- 2 tbsp. melted butter
- 1 tbsp. coarse salt
- 1 tbsp. poppy seeds (or everything seasoning)

Directions:

1. FOR OVEN
2. Preheat oven to 375°. Spray an 8" round baking pan or pie dish with cooking spray.
3. In a large nonstick skillet, melt butter over medium heat. In a large bowl, whisk together eggs and milk. Pour egg mixture in pan and let set slightly. Reduce heat to medium low, and stir occasionally until scrambled eggs reach desired consistency. Season with salt and pepper. Remove from heat and fold in chives.
4. Flatten each biscuit round to about ¼" thickness. Top each round of dough with scrambled eggs, bacon and cheese. Bring the edges of the dough together and pinch to seal. Place in pan seam side-down.
5. Brush with tops with melted butter then sprinkle with coarse salt and poppy seeds. Bake until the biscuits are golden and cooked through, about 20 to 25 minutes. Serve warm.
6. FOR AIR FRYER
7. In a large skillet over medium heat, melt butter. In a large bowl, whisk together eggs and milk. Pour egg mixture in pan and let set slightly. Reduce heat to medium-low, and stir occasionally until soft curds form. Season with salt and pepper. Remove from heat and fold in chives.
8. Flatten each biscuit into a ¼" thick round. Top each round of dough with scrambled eggs, bacon and cheese. Bring the edges of the dough together and pinch to seal.
9. Brush with tops with melted butter then sprinkle with salt and everything seasoning.
10. Line basket of air fryer with a piece of parchment paper greased with cooking spray and, working in batches, add biscuit bombs, making sure they don't touch. Bake at 375° until biscuits are golden and cooked through, about 10 minutes.

Air Fryer Egg Rolls

Servings: 12
Cooking Time: 12 Minutes

Ingredients:

- 2 Tablespoon vegetable oil
- 1/2 Teaspoon minced garlic
- 1/2 Teaspoon minced ginger
- 1/2 cup finely chopped celery
- 2 cups coleslaw mix
- 1/2 pound ground chicken
- 3 Tablespoon oyster sauce

- 1 Tablespoon soy sauce
- 1 Teaspoon toasted sesame oil
- 1 Tablespoon sriracha
- 1/2 cup chopped green onions
- 12 egg roll wrappers
- olive oil spray

Directions:

1. Heat oil in a pan and stir fry garlic, ginger, celery till fragrant. Add the coleslaw mix and cook till the cabbage is wilted.
2. Add the ground chicken, oyster sauce, soy sauce, sesame oil and sriracha. Stir fry the chicken while breaking it up for 3-4 minutes. Once the chicken is cooked and there is no liquid left in the pan, stir in the green onions and remove from stove.
3. To wrap the egg rolls, place the egg roll wrapper so that one corner is towards you. Place a tablespoon of filling in the bottom half (towards you) and wrap that corner over the filling. turn both sides over the wrapper and then continue rolling away from you (like a burrito), till you reach the end. Seal the edges with some water or a beaten egg. Repeat till all the wrappers are made.
4. Spray the basket of the air fryer with olive oil spray. Place the egg rolls in the basket and lightly spray the tops of the egg rolls with the olive oil spray. Cook at 400 degrees for 6 minutes. Then flip the egg rolls and cook for an additional 6 minutes.

Frozen Pot Pie In Air Fryer

Servings: 2
Cooking Time: 25 Minutes

Ingredients:

- 2 Frozen Pot Pies 10 ounce Chicken, Beef, or Veggie

Directions:

1. To make air fryer pot pie, begin by removing the pot pie from it's packaging and cover the pie with aluminum foil, folding the foil over the sides of pie.
2. Place the pot pie in the air fryer basket and air fry at 400 degrees F for 20-25 minutes.

3. Remove the foil, and continue to air fry for an additional 3-5 minutes, until you have golden brown crust.

Air Fryer Pop Tarts

Servings: 2-4
Cooking Time: 4 Minutes

Ingredients:

- 2 to 4 Pop Tarts (any flavor)

Directions:

1. Preheat your air fryer to 350 degrees.
2. Place your desired amount of pop tarts in the air fryer basket without overlapping them.
3. Cook for 3-4 minutes. Cook time may vary depending on the number of pop tarts in your basket and your air fryer design.
4. Remove carefully and enjoy.

Pumpkin Spice Loaf

Servings: 2

Ingredients:

- Pumpkin Spice Loaf:
- ¾ cup pumpkin puree
- 2 large eggs, room temperature
- ½ cup light olive oil
- ½ cup buttermilk
- 1 teaspoon vanilla extract
- ½ cup white sugar
- ½ cup brown sugar, packed
- 1¾ cups all-purpose flour
- 1 teaspoon baking soda
- ½ teaspoon salt
- ½ teaspoon cinnamon
- ½ teaspoon pumpkin pie spice
- ¼ teaspoon ginger
- ¼ teaspoon nutmeg
- Oil spray
- Maple Cream Cheese Glaze:

- 1 package cream cheese (8-ounces), room temperature
- ½ stick unsalted butter, room temperature
- ¾ cup powdered sugar
- ¼ cup pure maple syrup
- 1 teaspoon vanilla extract
- Pinch of salt
- Chopped pecans or pumpkin seeds, for topping
- Items Needed:
- 2 mini loaf pans
- Toothpicks
- Stand mixer with paddle attachment

Directions:

1. Whisk together the pumpkin puree, eggs, oil, buttermilk, vanilla extract, and both sugars until smooth.
2. Add the flour, baking soda, salt, cinnamon, pumpkin pie spice, ginger, and nutmeg. Stir with a spatula until combined.
3. Select the Preheat function on the Air Fryer, adjust temperature to 300°F, and press Start/Pause.
4. Grease 2 mini loaf pans with oil spray. Pour the batter into the loaf pans, filling each ⅔ full. Make any leftover batter into muffins, if desired.
5. Insert the loaf pans into the air fryer baskets.
6. Set temperature to 300°F and time to 32 minutes, then press Start/Pause.
7. Remove loaves when a toothpick inserted into the center of each comes out clean.
8. Allow loaves to cool to room temperature before glazing.
9. Beat the cream cheese and butter in a stand mixer until smooth. Add the powdered sugar, maple syrup, vanilla extract, and a pinch of salt. Beat until smooth.
10. Glaze the mini pumpkin spice loaves with the maple cream cheese glaze and top with chopped pecans or pumpkin seeds.

Shrimp Egg Rolls

Servings: 6
Cooking Time: 15 Minutes

Ingredients:

- 1 tablespoon toasted sesame oil
- 1 teaspoon grated ginger
- 3 garlic cloves (minced)
- 2 large scallions (chopped)
- 3 cups chopped green cabbage
- 1/2 cups shredded carrots
- 2 tablespoons reduced sodium soy sauce
- 1/2 tablespoon unseasoned rice vinegar
- 1/2 pound large peeled raw shrimp (chopped)
- 6 egg roll wrappers
- Olive oil spray
- Sweet chili sauce, duck sauce or spicy mustard (for dipping (optional))

Directions:

1. In a large skillet, heat sesame oil over medium-high heat. Add the shrimp and sauté, until shrimp is almost cooked through, 1 to 2 minutes.
2. Add ginger, garlic and scallions. Sauté until fragrant, about 30 seconds. Add cabbage and carrots, soy sauce and vinegar.
3. Cook on high heat until vegetables are tender crisp, about 2 to 3 minutes. Transfer to a colander to drain and let cool.
4. One at a time, place egg roll wrapper on a clean surface, points facing top and bottom like a diamond. Spoon a 1/3 cup mixture onto the bottom third of the wrapper.
5. Dip your finger in a small bowl of water and run it along the edges of the wrapper. Lift the point nearest you and wrap it around the filling.
6. Fold the left and right corners in toward the center and continue to roll into a tight cylinder. Set aside and repeat with remaining wrappers and filling.
7. Spray all sides of the egg rolls with oil using your fingers to evenly coat.

8. In batches, cook 370F for 5 to 7 minutes, turning halfway through until golden brown.
9. Serve immediately, with dipping sauce on the side, if desired.
10. To make this in the oven
11. Preheat oven to 425F, then stuff and bake until golden on both sides, 15 to 20 minutes.

Mom-osa French Toast

Servings: 4

Ingredients:
- French Toast:
- 3 large eggs
- 2 tablespoons honey
- ½ cup whole milk
- ½ cup heavy cream
- 2 teaspoons ground cinnamon
- ½ teaspoon kosher salt
- 4 slices thick-cut brioche bread, dried out (day-old bread)
- Oil spray
- Powdered sugar, for serving
- Raspberry Champagne Coulis:
- 1½ cups fresh or frozen raspberries
- 1¼ cups champagne
- ½ cup granulated sugar
- Orange Whipped Cream:
- Oil spray
- Oil spray
- Oil spray

- Items Needed:
- Electric mixer or stand mixer fitted with the whisk attachment

Directions:
1. Whip the heavy cream, orange zest, and powdered sugar in a medium bowl with an electric mixer or a stand mixer. Whisk for about 5 minutes or until stiff peaks form, then refrigerate for 15 minutes.
2. Add raspberries, champagne, and sugar into a small saucepan and cook for 15 minutes on low heat.
3. Strain the raspberry coulis through a mesh strainer, using a spoon to strain as much liquid and pulp as you can. Don't forget to scrape the bottom of the strainer for the pulp. Set aside to cool for about 10 minutes.
4. Whisk together the eggs, honey, milk, heavy cream, cinnamon, and salt until well combined.
5. Submerge the bread into the egg mixture for about 10 seconds.
6. Remove the crisper plate from the Smart Air Fryer basket.
7. Coat the basket with oil spray to prevent the toast from sticking.
8. Place the soaked bread directly into the air fryer basket and spray the tops of the toasts with oil spray.
9. Select the Air Fry function, adjust temperature to 375°F and time to 12 minutes, then press Start/Pause.
10. Remove the french toast when done, then serve topped with raspberry coulis and orange whipped cream and dust with powdered sugar.

DESSERTS RECIPES

Apple Cider Cupcakes With Apple Cider Cranberry Filling & Cinnamon Cream Frosting

Ingredients:

- For the Cupcake
- 2 eggs
- 1 2/3 cup flour
- 1 cup apple cider
- 2/3 cup sugar
- ½ cup butter
- 2 tsp baking powder
- 1 tsp cinnamon
- ½ tsp salt
- 1 tsp vanilla
- For the Frosting
- 1 package cream cheese
- ½ cup butter, softened
- 4 cups powdered sugar
- 1 tsp vanilla
- ½ Tbsp cinnamon
- For the Cranberry Filling
- 12oz bag fresh cranberries
- ¼ cup granulated sugar
- ¼ cup maple syrup
- ½ sweet apple, peeled and finely diced
- ½ cup apple cider
- 1 cinnamon stick

Directions:

1. For the Cupcakes
2. Cream together butter and sugar in a large mixing bowl using a hand mixer. Add the eggs and vanilla and mix until fully incorporated.
3. In a separate bowl, combine the dry ingredients together.
4. Alternating between apple cider and the dry mixture, slowly incorporate them into the butter/sugar/egg mixture.
5. Line cupcake tins with liners.
6. Fill cupcakes 2/3 and bake at 350 F for 15 minutes or until toothpick inserted into the center comes out clean. Let cool completely.
7. For the Frosting
8. Cream the cream cheese and butter together with a hand mixer for about 2 minutes, until light and fluffy.
9. Add vanilla and mix to combine.
10. Add half of the powdered sugar and half of the cinnamon. Cream mixture for about 1 minute. Then add the second half and cream until smooth.
11. Keep covered in the refrigerator until ready to frost.
12. For the Cranberry Filling
13. Place all ingredients in the heated blender.
14. Set to soup setting and let simmer for 15 minutes. Remove the cinnamon stick.
15. Hit the Chop button twice. Turn off the blander and let sit to cool.

Air Fryer Pumpkin Biscuits

Servings: 4

Ingredients:

- 1 c. all-purpose flour, plus more for surface
- 1 tbsp. light brown sugar
- 1 tsp. baking powder
- 3/4 tsp. pumpkin spice
- 1/2 tsp. kosher salt
- 4 tbsp. cold unsalted butter, cut into cubes, plus 1 tbsp. melted for brushing
- 1/4 c. canned pure pumpkin puree
- 2 tbsp. buttermilk

Directions:

1. In a medium bowl, whisk flour, sugar, baking powder, pumpkin spice, and salt. Using a fork or 2 table knives, work cubed butter into flour mixture until it resembles a coarse meal.
2. In a liquid measuring cup or another medium bowl, whisk pumpkin puree and buttermilk until

combined. Pour into flour mixture and stir with a fork until just combined and a shaggy dough forms.

3. Turn the dough out onto a lightly floured work surface. Gently knead dough with your hands until no dry spots remain. Pat dough into a 4"-by-4" square and cut into 4 squares. Brush tops of squares with melted butter.

4. In an air-fryer basket, arrange dough squares in a single layer. Cook at 350°, tenting with foil during the last 3 minutes to prevent overbrowning if necessary, until golden and risen, 10 to 12 minutes.

Air Fryer S'mores

Servings: 2

Ingredients:
- 2 graham crackers, halved
- 1 chocolate bar, halved
- 2 jumbo marshmallows, halved

Directions:
1. Preheat Air Fryer to 400°F (205°C).
2. Preheat graham cracker halves in the bottom of the air fryer basket.
3. Place the halved marshmallows, cut side down, in the center of the graham cracker.
4. Cook at 400F for 6 minutes, or until the tops of the marshmallows are nice and golden brown
5. Place a piece of chocolate on top of the marshmallows, followed by another half of the graham cracker. Serve immediately.

Grilled Peaches With Burrata

Ingredients:
- 3-4 peaches, sliced
- 1 cup Burrata cheese
- ½ cup balsamic vinegar
- 2 tbsp olive oil
- salt and pepper to taste
- fresh basil
- 2 cups arugula
- sliced baguette

Directions:

1. Pour 2 cups of water into your GoWISE USA Smokeless Grill drip tray. Set your grill to medium high and turn on the fan. Then, brush the sliced peaches with olive oil and grill on medium high for 6 minutes, flipping occasionally.

2. While the peaches are grilling, prepare the balsamic reduction. In a small saucepan, cook the balsamic vinegar over low heat until the vinegar has reduced to at least half the original amount.

3. Slice your baguette and place the sliced pieces on your grill. Brush them with olive oil and grill for 2 minutes on each side.

4. Add grilled peaches to a bed of arugula. Top with Burrata cheese and fresh basil and drizzle on the balsamic reduction. Season with salt and pepper to taste. Serve with toasted baguette slices and enjoy!

Air Fryer Fried Candy Bars

Servings: 8
Cooking Time: 7 Minutes

Ingredients:
- on (12-ounce) can refrigerated crescent dough sheets
- 8 miniature chocolate candy bars, chilled in refrigerator
- oil, for spraying
- powdered sugar

Directions:

1. Separate dough triangles, and wrap each triangle around one candy bar.

2. Working in batches of 4, spray wrapped candy bars with oil and place in air fryer basket. Set temperature to 375 degrees, and air fry for 5 minutes. Turn candy bars, spray with oil, and air fry for 2 minutes more, or until golden brown. Remove candy bars to a platter and immediately sprinkle with powdered sugar. Repeat with remaining candy bars. Serve warm.

Air Fryer Apple Fritters

Servings: 12
Cooking Time: 6 Minutes

Ingredients:

- 2 apples, cored and diced
- 1 cup all-purpose flour
- 2 tablespoons sugar
- 1 teaspoon baking powder
- 1/2 teaspoon salt
- 1/2 teaspoon ground cinnamon
- 1/4 teaspoon ground nutmeg
- 1/3 cup milk
- 2 tablespoons butter, melted
- 1 egg
- 1/2 teaspoon lemon juice
- CINNAMON GLAZE
- 1/2 cup confectioners sugar
- 2 tablespoons milk
- 1/2 teaspoon ground cinnamon
- Pinch of salt

Directions:

1. Dice the apples into small cubes and set aside. Peel them if desired.
2. Add the flour, sugar, baking powder, salt, ground cinnamon, and ground nutmeg into a large mixing bowl and stir to combine.
3. In a separate bowl, mix the milk, butter,* egg, and lemon juice.
4. Add the wet ingredients into the dry ingredients and stir just until combined. Stir in the apples and put mixture into the fridge for anywhere from 5 minutes to 2 days (covered).
5. Preheat your air fryer to 370 degrees.
6. Put a parchment round on the bottom of the basket and scoop out apple fritters into 2-tablespoon balls. Place apple fritters in the air fryer and cook for 6-7 minutes.
7. While cooking, whisk the confectioners sugar, milk, cinnamon, and salt together to make the glaze.
8. Remove the apple fritters from the air fryer, place them on a wire rack, and immediately pour the glaze over top and enjoy!

NOTES

*to make the apple fritters even fluffier, grate the butter in cold to the recipe instead of using melted butter.
HOW TO REHEAT APPLE FRITTERS IN THE AIR FRYER:
Preheat your air fryer to 320 degrees.
Cook apple fritters for 2-3 minutes and enjoy! If cooking from refrigerated, add 1-2 additional minutes.

Air Fryer Apple Tart

Servings: 6
Cooking Time: 20 Minutes

Ingredients:

- 2 Granny Smith apples peeled, cored, sliced
- 1/3 cup brown sugar
- 1/2 teaspoon cinnamon
- 1/2 teaspoon vanilla extract
- 1/2 teaspoon lemon juice
- 1/4 cup butter unsalted
- 1 refrigerated pie crust

Directions:

1. Prepare the tart pan with nonstick spray.
2. In a medium bowl, combine the melted butter, cinnamon, brown sugar, lemon, and vanilla extract. Set aside.
3. Unroll the refrigerated dough.
4. Press pie crust dough into the prepared tart pan.
5. Place the tart pan and pie crust into the basket of the air fryer. Poke holes into the crust with a fork before baking.
6. Air fry the pie crust at 320 degrees Fahrenheit for 4-5 minutes.
7. Carefully remove the tart pan.
8. Arrange the apples over the dough.
9. Brush the tops of the apples with melted butter, vanilla, cinnamon, lemon juice, and brown sugar.
10. Place the tart back into the basket of the air fryer.
11. Air fry at 320 degrees Fahrenheit for 16-20 minutes.
12. Allow the tart to cool slightly before slicing and serving.

NOTES

I was able to make a complete tart with just 2 apples. If you are using a larger tart pan, you may want to slice an additional apple.

While you don't have to have a mandolin for slicing apples thin, I prefer to use one so that my slices are an even thickness and will cook evenly.

This recipe was made in the 1700 watt 5.8 quart Cosori Air Fryer. If using a different air fryer brand, you may need to adjust the cooking time slightly because all air fryers cook differently.

Air Fryer Birthday Cake Cinnamon Rolls

Servings: 5

Ingredients:

- 1 can (17.5 oz) refrigerated Pillsbury™ Grands!™ Cinnamon Rolls with Original Icing (5 Count)
- 4 oz (from 8-oz package) cream cheese, softened
- 1/2 cup powdered sugar
- 5 cookie dough rounds from 1 package (16 oz) refrigerated Pillsbury™ Ready to Bake!™ Sugar Cookie Dough (24 Count)
- 1 tablespoon rainbow candy sprinkles

Directions:

1. Cut two 8-inch rounds of cooking parchment paper. Place one round in bottom of air fryer basket. Spray with cooking spray.
2. Separate dough into 5 rolls; set icing aside. Place 3 rolls on parchment paper in air fryer basket, spacing apart. Cover remaining rolls with plastic wrap, and refrigerate.
3. Set air fryer to 320°F; cook 12 minutes. Place a large plate over air fryer basket, and invert. Discard parchment. Carefully transfer cinnamon rolls back to air fryer, bottom side up. Cook 2 to 4 minutes or until golden brown and rolls are cooked thorough. Remove from air fryer; cover loosely with foil to keep warm while cooking second batch. Repeat for remaining 2 rolls, and place on remaining parchment round in basket of air fryer. Cook as directed above.

4. Meanwhile, in small bowl, place icing and cream cheese; beat with spoon until well blended. Stir in powdered sugar until mixed well. In another small bowl, crumble cookie dough rounds into small pieces. Add sprinkles, and stir until coated. Spread icing mixture on tops of warm cinnamon rolls; crumble sprinkled coated cookie dough pieces on tops. Serve warm.

Air Fryer Chocolate Cheesecake

Servings: 8
Cooking Time: 18 Minutes

Ingredients:

- Cheesecake Oreo Crust
- 30 cookies crushed
- 1/2 cup unsalted butter
- Cheesecake Filling
- 2 cups semi-sweet chocolate chips
- 24 ounces cream cheese (3-8 ounce packages)
- 1/2 cup powdered sugar
- 2 teaspoon cornstarch
- 2 large eggs
- 1 teaspoon vanilla

Directions:

1. Prepare the pan by lining the bottom with a circle of parchment paper, and then lightly butter the insides of the pan walls so the cheesecake will easily be removed after cooking.
2. Crush the Oreo Cookies in the food processor, until they are fine crumbs. (Or you can place them in a large bag and crush them with a rolling pin.
3. Pour the crushed cookies into a large bowl, and stir in the melted butter to mix with the crumbs.
4. Pour the mixture into the prepared springform pan, pressing the crust firmly to the bottom of the pan. Set the pan aside.
5. In a microwave safe bowl, melt the chocolate chips, stirring after one minute to make sure the chips have completely melted and are smooth. Set the bowl aside as you prepare the filling.

6. In a large bowl, or using a stand mixer, beat the cream cheese until it is smooth.

7. Add in the powdered sugar, corn starch, eggs, and vanilla. Quickly stir in the melted chocolate, until the filling is well combined and smooth. Pour the filling over the crust and spread it evenly with a spatula or spoon.

8. Place the springform pan in the basket of the air fryer. Cook at 300 degrees Fahrenheit for 18 minutes.

9. Remove from the basket and allow the cheesecake to chill to set, for about 6-8 hours, or chill in the freezer for about an hour.

NOTES

The cheesecake will be a little soft when it is done cooking. It will firm up once it cools. Be sure to line the pan, and then butter the sides of the wall of the pan.

The first time I made an air fryer cheesecake, I didn't butter the sides and the cheesecake stuck a little bit. If you forget, just slide a knife in between the cheesecake and the pan and go around until it is loosened.

Air Fryer Sweet Plantains

Servings: 1-2

Ingredients:

- 2 very ripe (blackened) plantains, halved lengthwise, peeled, then thinly sliced ¾"-thick on a bias
- 2 tsp. extra-virgin olive oil
- Kosher salt

Directions:

1. In a small bowl, toss plantains with oil. In an air-fryer basket, arrange plantains in a single layer. Cook at 370°, tossing halfway through, until golden and very tender, 12 to 14 minutes; season with salt.

Air Fryer Brie

Servings: 4
Cooking Time: 5 Minutes

Ingredients:

- 8 ounces Brie Cheese
- 2 tablespoons dried cranberries or cherries
- 2 tablespoons sliced almonds
- 1 tablespoon honey or flavored liqueur such as Chambord or Bailey's Irish Creme
- 1 small baguette sliced and toasted

Directions:

1. Prepare the cheese by removing the brie rind on top of the cheese wheel only. Leave the rind around the sides and bottom of the cheese.

2. Place cheese in a small ramekin or oven safe dish. Place brie in center or your basket. Air fry at 350 degrees F for 5-7 minutes until the cheese is soft and warm.

3. While cheese is in air fryer, in a small, microwave safe bowl, combine the cranberries, almonds, and honey or liquor. Stir together and then microwave for 30-45 seconds, until warm.

4. Pour ingredients over the top of the brie and serve while hot.

NOTES

Optional Flavors: spiced rum, fig jam, Cointreau, maple syrup, kalua, or berry cranberry sauce.

Optional Toppings: cranberry sauce, roasted mushrooms, drizzle of dark chocolate, tangy brie honey mixture, an artichoke-sundried tomato mixture, caramel sauce, crumbled air fryer bacon, air fryer candied chopped walnuts or pistachios.

Cooking Tips: Use a sharp knife to cut away rind on top of cheese so you keep as much cheese on the wheel to enjoy later.

Jam And Cream Doughnuts

Ingredients:
- ½ tsp salt
- ¼ cup sugar
- 4T butter, melted and cooled
- 1 large egg
- 3 cups flour
- 1 cup milk, warm
- 2 ½ tsp yeast
- 1 tsp vanilla essence
- Jam to serve
- Whipped cream to serve

Directions:
1. To make the dough, add a teaspoon of sugar, yeast, milk and vanilla essence, mix and allow to rest until bubbly. Add the remaining sugar, salt and egg to the yeast. Add the butter and two cups of flour, mix until smooth, add the last cup of flour and knead until smooth. Cover with cling wrap for 30 minuntes. Punch down dough and roll out to about 3cm thick then cut into 7cm rounds. Allow to rise for another 15 minutes on a greased tray.
2. While waiting to rise, grease tray with vege oil and set to Air Fry for 7 minutes at 180C to pre-heat. Then add the donuts carefully and turn halfway. Check they're done (if not allow another 2 / 3 minutes on Air Fry. Once done remove them and let them cool slightly. While warm, lather in melted butter then coat in sugar and fill with jam and cream.

Easy Air Fryer Donuts

Servings: 8
Cooking Time: 10-12 Minutes

Ingredients:
- 1/2 cup granulated sugar
- 1 tablespoon ground cinnamon
- 1 (16.3-ounce) can flaky large biscuits, such as Pillsbury Grands! Flaky Biscuits
- Olive oil spray or coconut oil spray
- 4 tablespoons unsalted butter, melted

Directions:
1. Line a baking sheet with parchment paper. Combine sugar and cinnamon in a shallow bowl; set aside.
2. Remove the biscuits from the can, separate them, and place them on the baking sheet. Use a 1-inch round biscuit cutter (or similarly-sized bottle cap) to cut holes out of the center of each biscuit.
3. Lightly coat an air fryer basket with olive or coconut oil spray (do not use nonstick cooking spray such as Pam, which can damage the coating on the basket).
4. Place 3 to 4 donuts in a single layer in the air fryer (they should not be touching). Close the air fryer and set to 350°F. Cook, flipping halfway through, until the donuts golden-brown, 5 to 6 minutes total. Transfer donuts place to the baking sheet. Repeat with the remaining biscuits. You can also cook the donut holes — they will take about 3 minutes total.
5. Brush both sides of the warm donuts with melted butter, place in the cinnamon sugar, and flip to coat both sides. Serve warm.

Easy Air-fryer Doughnuts

Servings: 8
Cooking Time: 20 Minutes

Ingredients:
- 2 cups self-raising flour
- 1 1/4 cups icing sugar mixture, sifted
- 1 cup Greek-style yoghurt
- 1 tbs milk
- 10 drops pink food colouring (to tint)
- 1 tbs bright sprinkles

Directions:
1. Place flour and 1/2 cup sugar in a large bowl. Add yoghurt and stir to combine. If dough is too sticky, knead in a little extra flour. Turn dough out onto a lightly floured surface and knead until smooth. Cut dough into 8 portions.
2. Roll dough portions into balls, then flatten slightly. Using floured hands, make a hole in the centre with your finger, then pull and stretch dough, while maintaining round shape, to form 9cm round doughnuts (centre hole should be about 4cm).

3. Preheat air fryer to 180°C for 3 minutes. Place half of the doughnuts in air-fryer basket. Cook for 8 minutes, turning halfway through, or until golden brown and cooked through. Transfer to a wire rack to cool. Repeat with remaining doughnuts.

4. Meanwhile, combine milk and remaining sugar in a medium bowl. Tint pink with food colouring. Dip surface of each doughnut in icing and return to wire rack, icing-side up. Scatter with sprinkles. Serve.

Air Fryer Caramilk Crumpet French Toast

Servings: 3
Cooking Time: 15 Minutes

Ingredients:

- 100g Caramilk chocolate, grated, plus extra to serve
- 6g salted butter, softened
- 6 round crumpets
- 2 eggs
- 1 tbsp milk
- 1/2 cup sweetened condensed milk
- Thickened cream, whipped
- Select all Ingredients:

Directions:

1. Line the base of an air fryer with foil, ensuring it comes at least 1 inch up the sides of the basket.
2. Combine Caramilk and butter in a bowl. Divide into 6 portions. Spread each portion over each crumpet. Cut each crumpet in half and sandwich together.
3. Whisk eggs with milk and 2 tbsp of sweetened condensed milk. Dip each crumpet sandwich in the egg mixture, coating well on all sides. Place in the air fryer basket. Repeat with remaining crumpet sandwiches. Pour over remaining sweetened condensed milk. Cook at 150C for 15 minutes or until crumpets are golden and caramelised.
4. To serve, grate over extra Caramilk and top with whipped cream.
5.

Banoffee Muffins

Servings: 12

Ingredients:

- 200g self-raising flour
- 1 tsp mixed spice
- ½ tsp salt
- 2 ripe bananas, approx. 320g with skins on
- 200g light brown sugar
- 100g vegetable oil
- 2 large eggs, beaten
- 1 tsp vanilla essence
- 50g chocolate chips
- 100g thick caramel or dulce de leche
- 12 dried banana chips to decorate

Directions:

1. Sift the flour, mixed spice and salt into bowl.
2. In a large mixing bowl, peel and mash the bananas until smooth. Mix in sugar, oil, eggs, vanilla essence and whisk together until the oil is incorporated.
3. Slowly add the dry ingredients to bananas and whisk continually to combine, stir in chocolate chips.
4. Without a crisper plate inserted. Place 6 double thickness muffin cases in each drawer, spoon mixture between the muffin cases filling 3/4 full. Select zone 1, select BAKE, set temperature to 160°C, and set time to 15 minutes. Select MATCH. Press the START/STOP button to begin cooking.
5. When zone 1 time reaches 5 minutes, check whether muffins are cooked through. Cooking is complete when a wooden skewer inserted in the centre comes out clean. Remove muffins from drawer and let cool on a wire rack for 5 minutes before serving. Top each muffin with a spoonful of caramel and a banana chip.

Bloody Witch Finger Cookies

Servings: 30

Ingredients:

- 16 ounce package pre-made sugar cookie dough
- 1 cup all-purpose flour
- 3 teaspoons water
- 5 Oreo cookies, ground up into crumbs in a food processor
- ½ cup raspberry jam
- ½ cup sliced almonds

Directions:

1. Place sugar cookie dough, flour, water, and ¼ cup of the Oreo cookie crumbs in a large bowl. Knead with your hands or in a stand mixer until all the ingredients are incorporated into the dough.
2. Take 1 ½ tablespoons of dough at a time and roll the dough between your palms into a 5-inch longer finger about ¼-inch thick. Firmly press a sliced almond into the end of each finger to make fingernails. Make several horizontal cuts in the center of each finger to make knuckles. Place fingers on a wax paper lined baking sheet.
3. Select the Preheat function on the Air Fryer, adjust temperature to 320°F, and press Start/Pause.
4. Place fingers into the preheated air fryer basket. You will need to work in batches.
5. Set the temperature to 320°F, time to 7 minutes, and press Start/Pause.
6. Remove fingers when lightly golden and place on a wire rack to cool completely.
7. Heat the raspberry jam in a saucepan or microwave until gently warmed through.
8. Dip the end of each finger into the raspberry jam and place onto a serving platter.

Air Fryer Heart Shaped Whoopie Pies

Ingredients:

- 1 package of strawberry or red velvet cake mix
- 3 large eggs
- ½ cup canola oil
- 1/2 cup water
- 2 tsp vanilla extract
- 8 oz cream cheese
- ½ cup butter, softened
- 2 cups confectioners' sugar
- 1 cup miniature semisweet chocolate chips

Directions:

1. In a large bowl, combine cake mix, eggs, oil, and vanilla extract. Stir until combined.
2. Fill greased ramekins ¾ of the way full with batter.
3. Bake at 350°F for 25 minutes. Allow cakes to cool before removing them from ramekins.
4. For filling, beat cream cheese and butter together in a large bowl until blended. Gradually beat in confectioners' sugar until smooth. Stir in chocolate chips.
5. Cut the top layers off the cakes. Cut the remaining cake in half and fill with filling mixture. Decorate the tops as desired – we used a heart shaped cookie cutter and some sprinkles. Enjoy!

Crab Cakes

Servings: 8

Ingredients:
- Rémoulade
- ¼ cup mayonnaise
- 1 teaspoon capers, washed & drained
- ½ tablespoon sweet pickles, minced
- ½ tablespoon red onion, finely diced
- ½ tablespoon lemon juice
- ½ teaspoon Dijon mustard
- Salt & pepper, to taste
- Crab Cakes
- 1 large egg, beaten

- 1¼ tablespoons mayonnaise
- ¾ teaspoon Dijon mustard
- 1 teaspoon Worcestershire sauce
- 1 teaspoon Old Bay seasoning
- ¼ teaspoon salt
- A pinch white pepper
- ¼ cup celery, finely diced
- ¼ cup red bell pepper, finely diced
- 2 tablespoons fresh parsley, finely chopped
- ½ pound lump crab meat
- ⅓ cup panko breadcrumbs
- Cooking Spray

Directions:

1. MIX together rémoulade ingredients until everything is well incorporated. Set aside.
2. WHISK together the egg, mayonnaise, mustard, Worcestershire, Old Bay, salt, white pepper, cayenne pepper, celery, bell pepper, and parsley.
3. GENTLY FLAKE the crab meat into the egg mixture and fold together until well mixed.
4. SPRINKLE the breadcrumbs over the crab mixture and fold gently until breadcrumbs are well incorporated.
5. FORM the crab mixture into 4 cake patties and chill in the fridge for 30 minutes.
6. SELECT Preheat on the Air Fryer and press Start/Pause.
7. LINE the preheated inner basket with a sheet of parchment paper. Spray the crab cakes with cooking spray and lay them gently onto the paper.
8. COOK the crab cakes at 400°F for 8 minutes until golden brown.
9. FLIP the crab cakes halfway through cooking.
10. SERVE with the rémoulade.

Air Fryer Molten Chocolate Pots

Servings: 4
Cooking Time: 10-15 Minutes

Ingredients:
- 200g dark chocolate
- 100g butter
- 100g castor sugar
- 3 eggs
- 2 Tbsp flour
- 4-6 Tbsp Caramel Treat/Dulce De Leche (optional)
- Pinch of flaked sea salt
- Crème fraîche /Ice cream/ Cream for serving

Directions:

1. Melt the butter and chocolate together in a microwave, stirring every 30 seconds. Once fully melted and combined, set aside.
2. Whisk the eggs and sugar together. Slowly drizzle the hot chocolate mixture into the eggs whisking constantly to stop the eggs from scrambling. Add the flour. Once well combined, divide the Mixture between 4 or 6 oven safe ramekins (yield will vary depending on your ramekins). If adding dulce de leche, spoon this into the middle of each pudding, and cover it with a little of the batter.
3. Sprinkle a little flaked sea salt over the top of the pots (optional)
4. Preheat the Instant Pot Vortex or Duo Crisp to 190C on the bake setting.
5. Bake the molten pots for 9-10 minutes (small ramekins) or 13-14 minutes (larger ramekins) until the top is set, but the middle is still gooey.
6. Serve immediately with creme fraîche/ cream or ice cream.
7. Chefs Tip: If you'd prefer this dish to be gluten free, you can leave out the flour. This will change the cosnsistency/texture but only slightly.

POULTRY RECIPES

Chicken Fajitas With Spicy Potatoes

Servings: 4

Ingredients:

- 3 chicken breats
- 1 tbsp smoked paprika
- 1 tbsp ground coriander
- 1 tsp ground cumin
- 1 tsp garlic powder
- 1/2 tsp dried chilli flakes
- 1 tsp dried oregano
- 4 tbsp olive oil
- 1 juice of lime
- salt and freshly ground black pepper
- 1 onion, peeled and sliced
- 1 red pepper, de-seeded and sliced
- 1 yellow pepper, de-seeded and sliced
- 8 medium tortillas
- For the spicy potatoes
- 1kg baby potatoes, cut in quarters
- 3 tbsp olive oil
- 2 tsp hot paprika
- 1 tbsp garlic powder
- 1 tbsp smoked paprika
- 1 tsp sea salt
- COOKING MODE
- When entering cooking mode - We will enable your screen to stay 'always on' to avoid any unnecessary interruptions whilst you cook!

Directions:

1. Slice chicken breasts into thin strips.
2. Add spices, herbs, lime juice and oil into a large bowl, season to taste and mix together.
3. Stir in chicken pieces, onion and peppers, mix all together until everything is coated in the marinade.
4. In another bowl, toss potatoes in oil and spices
5. Insert a crisper plate in both drawers. Add chicken and vegetables to zone 1 drawer and potatoes to zone 2 drawer and insert into unit.
6. Select zone 1, select AIR FRY, set temperature to 200°C and set time to 20 minutes. Select zone 2 and select ROAST, set temperature to 180°C and set time to 25 minutes. Select SYNC. Select START/STOP to begin.
7. After 10 minutes, give both drawers a shake or stir. Repeat again after 15 minutes.
8. When zone 1 time reaches 0, check chicken is cooked. Cooking is complete when the internal temperature reaches at least 75°C on an instant read thermometer.
9. Serve chicken and vegetables wrapped in the tortillas with the potatoes on the side.

Greek Lemon Chicken Wings In The Air Fryer

Ingredients:

- 10-12 chicken wings
- 1/2 cup extra virgin olive oil
- 1/2 cup lemon juice
- 6 garlic cloves, minced
- 1 ½ Tbsp. dried oregano
- 1 Tbsp. black pepper
- 1/2 Tbsp. Salt
- 1 tsp paprika
- 1 tsp cayenne pepper
- Crumbled feta cheese, for garnish
- Sliced lemons, for garnish
- For the Tzatziki
- 1 cup Greek yogurt
- 2 cloves garlic, minced
- 2 tablespoons chopped fresh dill
- 1 English cucumber, grated and drained

- Salt and pepper, to taste

Directions:

1. For the marinade, whisk together the extra virgin olive oil, lemon juice, oregano, salt, pepper, paprika, cayenne and garlic.
2. Add the chicken wings to a Ziploc bag and toss to coat the wings evenly. Refrigerate for about 30 minutes-1 hour.
3. Spray your air fryer's basket with nonstick cooking spray and add in the wings.
4. Air fry at 400F for 24 minutes, flipping the wings throughout the cooking cycle to get an even crisp.
5. While your wings are cooking, make the Tzatziki by adding the greek yogurt, garlic, dill, cucumber, salt and pepper to a small bowl. Refrigerate until ready to serve.
6. Transfer the chicken wings to a serving bowl or platter. Garnish with feta cheese, lemon slices, and the Tzatziki sauce. Enjoy!

Air Fryer Chicken Legs

Servings: 4
Cooking Time: 30 Minutes

Ingredients:

- 3-4 chicken legs
- 1 tablespoon olive oil
- 1 tablespoon chicken seasoning* see note
- ½ teaspoon garlic powder
- salt & pepper to taste

Directions:

1. Preheat air fryer to 370°F.
2. Pat chicken dry with a paper towel. Drizzle olive oil over chicken legs and generously season with chicken seasoning, garlic powder, and salt & pepper to taste.
3. Place the chicken legs in a single layer in the air fryer basket, skin side down, and cook for 20 minutes.
4. Flip the legs over and cook an additional 5-10 minutes or until the legs reach 165°F.

NOTES
*Premade chicken seasonings can vary in flavor and salt level. Season to taste or preference.
Homemade Chicken Seasoning
1 teaspoon paprika
1/2 teaspoon garlic powder
1/2 teaspoon kosher salt, more or less to taste
1/4 teaspoon black pepper
1/4 teaspoon dried thyme leaves
Ensure legs aren't too crowded so air can circulate around them. Do not overlap.

Air Fryer Bbq Chicken Wings

Servings: 4
Cooking Time: 20 Minutes

Ingredients:

- 24 chicken wings
- 1 Tbsp garlic powder
- 2 Tbsp brown sugar
- 2/3 cup BBQ sauce

Directions:

1. Preheat the Air Fryer to 380 degrees Fahrenheit. Prepare the Air Fryer basket with olive oil spray, nonstick cooking spray, or parchment paper AFTER you've preheated the Air Fryer.
2. Rinse and completely dry the chicken wings.
3. Mix the garlic powder and brown sugar together and use as a dry rub over the wings. For extra crispy wings, add a pinch of baking powder to the seasoning before coating the wings.
4. Place the wings in a single layer in the basket of the air fryer.
5. Cook the wings at 380 degrees Fahrenheit for 16 minutes, flipping the ings every 4 minutes. Increase the heat to 400 degrees Fahrenheit and cook for an additional 4 minutes. Use a meat thermometer to ensure the wings have reached 165 degrees Fahrenheit. Add 1-2 minutes time if needed.
6. Remove the chicken wings from the air fryer and place them into a medium sized mixing bowl. Cover

the wings with BBQ sauce and then toss the wings until they are completely coated in sauce.

7. Serve with your favorite sides and dipping sauces.

NOTES

Serve the wings with more BBQ sauce or your favorite dipping sauces, such as honey mustard or creamy Ranch dressing.

Add a pinch of baking powder to the seasoning to make the wings extra crispy on the outside.

Weight Watchers approx 6-8 points per 4 oz serving of wings

Air Fryer Chicken Parmesan Meatballs

Servings: 4
Cooking Time: 15 Minutes

Ingredients:

- 1 lb ground chicken breast
- 1 cup breadcrumbs
- 1 egg
- 1 Tbsp Italian seasoning
- 1 tsp ground black pepper
- 1/2 cup parmesan cheese
- 3/4 cup marinara sauce
- 1/2 cup shredded mozzarella cheese

Directions:

1. Mix the chicken, breadcrumbs, paremsan cheese, egg, and seasoning in a small mixing bowl.
2. Prepare the air fryer basket with a piece of parchment paper or nonstick cooking spray.
3. Roll the chicken mixture into nine 2" meatballs.
4. Place the meatballs onto the prepared Air Fryer basket in a single layer, leaving room in between the meatballs. (Do not preheat the air fryer for this recipe.)
5. Cook on 350 degrees Fahrenheit for 12 minutes, flipping the meatballs halfway through. Add marinara sauce on top of each chicken meatball and then top with mozzarella cheese. Cook on 350 for an additional 2 minutes.

6. Serve over noodles, in a hoagie bun, on sliders, or as an appetizer.

NOTES

Store leftover meatballs in an airtight container for up to 3 days.

Reheat the meatballs in the Air Fryer at 350 degrees for 2-3 minutes until warmed to your liking.

Serve chicken parmesan meatballs on a bed of spaghetti, a hoagie roll, on sliders, or alone as an appetizer.

Air Fryer Honey Soy Chicken Thighs

Servings: 4
Cooking Time: 10 Minutes

Ingredients:

- 1.5lbs boneless skinless chicken thighs (can use up to 3lbs)
- HONEY SOY MARINADE
- 1/3 cup soy sauce
- 1/4 cup oil (I use vegetable oil)
- 3 tablespoons honey
- 1/2 teaspoon garlic powder
- 1/4 teaspoon ground ginger
- salt and pepper to taste

Directions:

1. Mix together the soy sauce*, oil, honey, garlic powder, and ground ginger in a big bowl.
2. Remove half of the marinade and place in a small bowl or container and set aside.
3. Add chicken thighs to a big bowl of marinade and coat chicken.
4. Refrigerate marinated chicken for at least 30 minutes or up to overnight.**
5. Preheat air fryer to 400 degrees.
6. Add marinated chicken to the air fryer and cook 10-15 minutes, until its internal temperature reaches 165 degrees.
7. Baste additional reserved sauce on top after cooking.
8. Enjoy immediately.

NOTES

*if using a low-sodium soy sauce, add a pinch of salt to up the flavor

**chicken can be made without being marinated, but may not lock all the honey soy flavor in.

HOW TO MAKE FROZEN CHICKEN THIGHS IN THE AIR FRYER:

Preheat your air fryer to 380 degrees.

Place frozen chicken thighs in the air fryer and cook for 15-20 minutes, depending on size. Flip them and baste them with half of the marinade halfway through cooking.

Remove them from the air fryer and baste them with remaining marinade, then enjoy!

Air Fryer Cornish Hen Recipe

Servings: 2-4
Cooking Time: 35-40 Minutes

Ingredients:

- 2 (1 to 1 1/4-pound) Cornish hens
- 1/2 small lemon
- 2 large sprigs fresh rosemary
- 1 teaspoon kosher salt
- 3/4 teaspoon poultry seasoning, or 1/2 teaspoon ground sage plus 1/4 teaspoon dried thyme
- 3/4 teaspoon garlic powder
- 3/4 teaspoon onion powder
- 3/4 teaspoon sweet paprika
- 1/2 teaspoon freshly ground black pepper
- 1/4 teaspoon granulated sugar
- 3 tablespoons olive oil, divided
- 2 slices bacon (optional)

Directions:

1. Pat 2 Cornish hens dry with paper towels, including behind the wings, legs, and inside the cavity. Place on a wire rack fitted over a large plate. Refrigerate uncovered for at least 1 hour, or up to overnight to dry the exterior and help create crispy skin.
2. Heat an air fryer to 380°F for 10 minutes. Meanwhile, prepare the following: Cut 1/2 small lemon in half again to create 2 quarters and remove any visible seeds. Cut 1 of the large rosemary sprigs in half crosswise. Place 1 teaspoon kosher salt, 3/4 teaspoon poultry seasoning, 3/4 teaspoon garlic powder, 3/4 teaspoon onion powder, 3/4 teaspoon paprika, 1/2 teaspoon black pepper, and 1/4 teaspoon granulated sugar in a small bowl and stir to combine.
3. Pat the Cornish hens dry again with paper towels. Rub 1 tablespoon of the olive oil on each hen, including the underside, wings, and thighs. Sprinkle 1/2 teaspoon of the spice mixture inside each the cavity of each hen. Sprinkle the outside of the hens with the remaining spice mixture, liberally rubbing the spices into the oil to create an even coating so that there are no spice clumps, which will burn in the air fryer. Place 1 lemon quarter and half a rosemary sprig inside each cavity. Wrap 1 slice bacon lengthwise over the center of each hen, and secure with a toothpick underneath, if using.
4. Brush the air fryer basket with a very thin layer of the remaining 1 tablespoon olive oil, reserving the rest. Carefully place both hens in the air fryer basket breast-side down. If you have a small basket, alternate the direction of the hens, so they face each other to ensure they snugly fit in the basket. You may need to use tongs to arrange the hens in the basket. Drizzle any remaining olive oil over both hens.
5. Air fry for 20 mintutes. Flip the hens and continue air frying until an instant-read thermometer registers 165°F in the thickest part of the thigh, 15 to 20 minutes more. Meanwhile, pick the leaves from the remaining large rosemary sprig and finely chop until you have about 1 teaspoon.
6. Transfer the Cornish hens from the air fryer with tongs to a large plate or clean cutting board. Let rest for 10 minutes. Discard any toothpicks and garnish with the chopped rosemary. Remove the lemon wedge from the cavity with a fork and carefully squeeze the juice over the Cornish hen if desired.

NOTES

Cornish hens: Cornish hens can range from 1 pound to 2 pounds; for air frying, the smaller size (1 to 1 1/4 pounds) is better, as you can fit two hens in the basket. If you can only get the larger 2-pound Cornish hens (which can be shared between two people), the cooking time will be longer if cooking two larger hens at once (if they can fit in your basket). Start checking the internal temperature after 30 minutes. If you have an air fryer with a small basket, you may only be able to fit one 2-pound hen in at once.

To serve a larger 2-pound hen to share, use kitchen shears to cut each hen in half down the breast bone and along the backbone.

Storage: Leftovers can be refrigerated in an airtight container for up to 4 days.

Teba Shio Chicken Wings

Servings: 3-4

Ingredients:

- ¾ cup cooking sake
- 1 pound chicken wings
- 1 teaspoon kosher salt
- 2 teaspoons Shichimi togarashi, plus more for serving
- ¼ teaspoon freshly ground white pepper
- 1 teaspoon grapeseed oil
- ½ teaspoon lemon juice
- Oil spray
- Lemon wedges, for serving

Directions:

1. Place the sake and chicken wings into a resealable plastic bag.
2. Marinate the chicken wings in the refrigerator for 20 minutes, ensuring they are fully submerged.
3. Remove the chicken wings and pat dry with paper towels.
4. Season the wings with salt, Shichimi togarashi, white pepper, grapeseed oil, and lemon juice.
5. Select the Preheat function on the Air Fryer, adjust temperature to 380°F, then press Start/Pause.

6. Spray the preheated inner basket with oil spray, then place the chicken wings into the preheated air fryer.
7. Select the Chicken function, adjust time to 18 minutes, press Shake, then press Start/Pause.
8. Flip the chicken wings halfway through cooking. The Shake Reminder will let you know when.
9. Remove when done and serve with Shichimi togarashi and lemon wedges.

Extra-crispy Air Fryer Chicken Wings

Servings: 4-6

Ingredients:

- 2 lb. chicken wings, flats and drumettes separated
- 1½ tsp. baking powder
- 1½ tsp. cornstarch
- Nonstick vegetable oil spray
- 1½ tsp. Diamond Crystal or 1 tsp. Morton kosher salt
- 1 tsp. freshly ground pepper
- 1 tsp. garlic salt
- 1 tsp. onion powder
- 1 tsp. smoked paprika
- 2 Tbsp. extra-virgin olive oil
- 2 Tbsp. mild hot sauce (preferably Frank's RedHot)
- Store-bought or homemade ranch dressing or blue cheese dressing (for serving)
- SPECIAL EQUIPMENT
- An air fryer

Directions:

1. Pat dry 2 lb. chicken wings, flats and drumettes separated, with paper towels and place in a medium bowl. Add 1½ tsp. baking powder and 1½ tsp. cornstarch; toss wings to coat. Transfer to a baking sheet or large plate and chill 1 hour.
2. Spray air-fryer basket with nonstick vegetable oil spray and heat air fryer to 400°. Mix 1½ tsp. Diamond Crystal or 1 tsp. Morton kosher salt, 1 tsp.

freshly ground pepper, 1 tsp. garlic salt, 1 tsp. onion powder, and 1 tsp. smoked paprika in a small bowl.

3. Transfer chicken wings to a clean large bowl. Sprinkle spice mixture over, then add 2 Tbsp. extra-virgin olive oil and 2 Tbsp. mild hot sauce (preferably Frank's RedHot) and toss wings to coat.

4. Working in 2 batches, arrange wings in a single layer in air fryer, spacing about ½" apart. Cook chicken wings, turning halfway through, until cooked through and golden brown and crisp, 25–30 minutes.

5. Transfer chicken wings to a platter and let rest 5 minutes. Serve with store-bought or homemade ranch dressing or blue cheese dressing.

Air Fryer Chicken Breast

Servings: 4
Cooking Time: 20-22 Minutes

Ingredients:

- 1 tablespoon Italian seasoning
- 1 1/2 teaspoons kosher salt
- 1 teaspoon garlic powder
- 1 teaspoon paprika
- 4 boneless, skinless chicken breasts (8 to 10 ounces each)
- 1 tablespoon olive oil

Directions:

1. Heat an air fryer to 400°F or 425°F. Place 1 tablespoon Italian seasoning, 1 1/2 teaspoons kosher salt, 1 teaspoon garlic powder, and 1 teaspoon paprika in a small bowl and stir to combine.

2. Coat 4 boneless, skinless chicken breasts with 1 tablespoon olive oil. Sprinkle the seasoning mixture over all sides of the chicken.

3. Use tongs to transfer the chicken to the air fryer and place in a single layer, working in batches if needed. If air frying at 400°F, air fry for 15 minutes. Flip the chicken and air fry for 13 to 15 minutes more. Alternatively, air fry at 425°F for 10 minutes.

Flip the chicken and air fry for 10 to 12 minutes more. The chicken is done when it registers 165°F on an instant-read thermometer inserted into the thickest part.

4. Transfer the chicken to a clean cutting board and let rest for 5 minutes before serving.

NOTES

Storage: Refrigerate leftovers in an airtight container for up to 4 days.

Air Fryer Chicken Drumsticks

Servings: 6
Cooking Time: 13 Minutes

Ingredients:

- 6 chicken drumsticks
- 2 teaspoons baking powder
- 1 teaspoon smoked paprika
- 2 teaspoons Italian seasonings
- 1 teaspoon garlic powder
- 1 teaspoon onion powder
- 1 teaspoon brown sugar
- 2 tablespoons olive oil

Directions:

1. Preheat the air fryer to 200C/400F.
2. In a small bowl, add the spices and mix well.
3. Pat dry the chicken drumsticks. Toss the drumsticks through the spice mix then drizzle the oil all over.
4. Place the drumsticks in the air fryer basket and cook for 8 minutes, flip, and cook for a further 6-8 minutes, or until cooked and crispy.
5. Serve immediately with your favorite sides.

NOTES

TO STORE: Leftovers can be stored in an air-tight container in the refrigerator for 4-5 days.

TO FREEZE: Air fryer chicken drumsticks can be frozen in a ziplock bag for up to 3 months.

TO REHEAT: Either microwave them for 20-30 seconds or reheat in the air fryer until crispy.

Turkey Bacon In The Air Fryer

Servings: 12
Cooking Time: 8 Minutes

Ingredients:

- 24 slices Turkey bacon (1 average package)

Directions:

1. Preheat air fryer to 390 degrees F (199 degrees C) for 5 minutes.
2. Add 5-6 slices of bacon to the air fryer basket in a single layer, without overlapping (or just barely at most).
3. Cook turkey bacon in the air fryer for 4 minutes.
4. Flip the bacon and spread out to ensure the pieces are not touching (they will have shrunk a bit from their original size). Cook for an additional 4-5 minutes, until crispy. (Bacon will crisp up more as it cools.)
5. Repeat steps 2-3 with the remaining bacon.

Actually Crispy Oven Baked Wings

Servings: 4
Cooking Time: 40 Minutes

Ingredients:

- 1 ½ pounds chicken wings split and tips removed, about 18 wings
- 1 tablespoon flour
- 1 teaspoon baking powder
- ½ teaspoon seasoned salt
- ½ teaspoon black pepper
- 1 tablespoon olive oil

Directions:

1. Pat wings dry with a paper towel.
2. Prepare a pan by lining with foil and placing a baking rack on it. Spray the rack with cooking spray.
3. Combine flour, baking powder, salt and pepper. Toss with wings and place on prepared pan.

Refrigerate 30 minutes (or up to 4 hours) uncovered.
4. Preheat oven to 425°F.
5. Toss wings with olive oil in a bowl (ensuring there are no dry spots of flour) and return back to the prepared pan.
6. Bake wings 20 minutes, flip and bake an additional 15 minutes. If your wings are smoking, remove the foil and add new foil. Cook until crisp and broil 1 minute each side if desired.
7. Toss with sauce or serve with dips.

NOTES

Pat the wings dry, moisture makes them steam (not crisp).

Don't skip the resting period, this allows them to dry out and to draw moisture from the skin.

Toss with olive oil for a little bit of crisp without the deep fry.

Place on a rack on your baking pan, this allows air to circulate all around the wings.

Line the pan with foil for easy clean up. If the pan begins to smoke from the drippings, add a new sheet of foil on top of the old foil.

For an extra-crisp, put the baked wings under the broiler for about 2 minutes until the skins start to become golden brown.

Ninja Foodi Chicken Thighs

Servings: 4
Cooking Time: 12 Minutes

Ingredients:

- 4 boneless skinless chicken thighs (you can use skin-on as well)
- 1 teaspoon salt
- 1 1/2 teaspoon brown sugar
- 1/2 teaspoon smoked paprika
- 1/2 teaspoon black pepper
- 1/2 cup BBQ sauce

Directions:

1. Preheat the Ninja Foodi to 375 degrees on Air Crisp.

2. Season the chicken by rubbing the salt, brown sugar, smoked paprika, and black pepper all over the chicken thighs.

3. Place the chicken thighs in the air fryer basket in a single layer and cook on Air Crisp for 10 minutes, flipping the chicken thighs halfway through cooking.

4. Remove the basket from the base and baste chicken with BBQ sauce on both sides. Place chicken thighs back in the air fryer and cook on Air Crisp for an additional 2 to 4 minutes.

5. Remove them from the air fryer and enjoy! Chicken thighs are done cooking once they reach an internal temperature of 165 degrees.

NOTES

HOW TO REHEAT CHICKEN THIGHS IN THE NINJA FOODI:

Preheat your Ninja Foodi on Air Crisp to 350 degrees. Cook leftover chicken thighs for about 3 minutes until warmed thoroughly.

HOW TO COOK FROZEN CHICKEN THIGHS IN THE NINJA FOODI:

Preheat your Ninja Foodi air fryer to 380 degrees on Air Crisp.

Rub the frozen chicken with the spice mixture in above recipe using a little oil if needed.

Cook the chicken thighs for 15 to 20 minutes, flipping the chicken halfway through.

Baste chicken with BBQ sauce on both sides, then cook for an additional 2 to 4 minutes.

Buffalo Pumpkin Spice Chicken Wings

Ingredients:

- 4 tsp Frank's RedHot® Original Seasoning Blend
- 1 Tbsp brown sugar
- 1 Tbsp Pumpkin Pie Spice
- 1 1/2 tsp Onion Powder
- 3/4 tsp Ground Mustard
- 1/2 tsp Garlic Powder
- 1 1/2 tsp salt

- 10-12 chicken wings
- 2 Tbsp pure maple syrup
- 2 tsp olive oil

Directions:

1. Mix RedHot Original Seasoning, brown sugar, pumpkin pie spice, onion powder, ground mustard, garlic powder and salt in small bowl. Place wings in large bowl. Add oil and 1/2 of the seasoning mixture; toss to coat. Arrange wings in single layer inside your air fryer basket.

2. Cook at 360 F for 24 minutes, flipping the wings over halfway, or until wings are cooked through and skin is crispy.

3. Mix the remaining seasoning mixture and maple syrup in large bowl. Add hot cooked wings; toss to coat. Serve immediately. Enjoy!

Air Fryer Chicken, Broccoli, And Onions

Servings: 4
Cooking Time: 20 Minutes

Ingredients:

- 1 pound (454 g) boneless skinless chicken breast or thighs , cut into 1-inch bites sized pieces
- 1/4-1/2 pound (113-227 g) broccoli , cut into florets (1-2 cups)
- 1/2 onion , sliced thick
- 3 Tablespoons (45 ml) vegetable oil or grape seed oil
- 1/2 teaspoon (2.5 ml) garlic powder
- 1 Tablespoon (15 ml) fresh minced ginger
- 1 Tablespoon (15 ml) soy sauce , or to taste (use Tamari for Gluten Free)
- 1 Tablespoon (15 ml) rice vinegar (use distilled white vinegar for Gluten Free)
- 1 teaspoon (5 ml) sesame oil
- 2 teaspoons (10 ml) hot sauce (optional)
- 1/2 teaspoon (2.5 ml) sea salt , or to taste
- black pepper , to taste

- serve with lemon wedges , optional

Directions:

1. AIR FRYING OPTION #1: REGULAR COOKED BROCCOLI

2. Make Marinade: In a bowl, combine oil, garlic powder, ginger, soy sauce, rice vinegar, sesame oil, optional hot sauce, salt, and pepper.

3. In bowl add chicken. In a second bowl add broccoli and onions. Divide the marinade between the two bowls, stirring to coat each completely.

4. Air Fry: Add just the chicken to the air fryer basket/tray. Air Fry at 380°F/195°C for 10 minutes. Stir in the broccoli and onions with the chicken (make sure to include all the marinade). Continue to Air Fry at 380°F/195°C for 8-10 minutes, or until the chicken is cooked through. Make sure to stir halfway through cooking so broccoli gets cooked evenly.

5. Season with additional salt and pepper, to taste. Add fresh lemon juice on top (optional) and serve warm.

6. AIR FRYING OPTION #2: EXTRA CRISPY, CHARRED BROCCOLI

7. Combine chicken, broccoli and onion in bowl. Toss ingredients together.

8. Make Marinade: In a bowl, combine oil, garlic powder, ginger, soy sauce, rice vinegar, sesame oil, optional hot sauce, salt, and pepper. Add the chicken, broccoli and onions to the marinade. Stir thoroughly to combine the marinade with chicken, broccoli and onions.

9. Air Fry: Add ingredients to air fryer basket/tray. Air Fry 380°F/195°C for 16-20 minutes, shaking and gently tossing halfway through cooking. Make sure to toss so that everything cooks evenly. Check chicken to make sure it's cooked through. If not, cook for additional 3-5 minutes.

10. If needed, season with additional salt and pepper, to taste. Add fresh lemon juice on top (optional) and serve warm.

NOTES

Air Frying Tips and **NOTES**:Shake or turn as directed in the recipe. Don't overcrowd the air fryer basket.Recipes were tested in 3.4 to 6 qt air fryers. If using a larger air fryer, the recipe might cook quicker so adjust cooking time.Remember to set a timer to shake/flip/toss as directed in recipe.

Air Fryer Rotisserie Chicken

Servings: 4
Cooking Time: 1 Hour

Ingredients:

- 2 teaspoons Kosher salt
- 1/2 teaspoon sweet paprika
- 1/2 teaspoon garlic powder
- 1/2 teaspoon onion powder
- 1/4 teaspoon dried oregano
- 1/4 teaspoon dried thyme
- 1/4 teaspoon ground sage
- olive oil spray
- 3 pounds whole chicken (I buy organic, humane raised)

Directions:

1. Combine the spices in a small bowl.

2. Spritz the chicken with olive oil and rub the spices all over, evenly.

3. Optional: For a prettier bird, tightly tie the legs of the chicken together with a piece of butcher's twine. At this point you can refrigerate uncovered until ready to cook.

4. When ready to cook, transfer the chicken to the air fryer basket.

5. Place the whole chicken in the air fryer, belly side down and air fry 350F about 25 minutes, until the top of the chicken is browned. Then flip over, and continue cooking about 25 minutes, or until the juices run clear and no longer pink when the thigh is pierced with a pairing knife near the joint, and the internal temperature is 165°F. For a larger bird, this will take more time. (Insert thermometer between the thickest part of the leg and the thigh)

6. When the chicken's done, remove it to a platter and let it rest for 10 minutes before carving and serving. Save carved carcass for stock if desired.

7. Serve the chicken, skin is optional.

8. No Air Fryer! No Problem (Oven Version)

9. To bake in the oven, bake 400F until golden and crisp and brown all over and the juices run clear when you insert a knife down to the bone between the leg and the thigh, or the internal temperature is 165°F, about 1 hour or longer as needed.

Garlicky Wings And Shishito Peppers

Servings: 4

Ingredients:

- 3 tbsp. fish sauce, divided
- 2 tbsp. lime juice, divided
- 1 tbsp. plus 1 teaspoon packed brown sugar, divided
- 4 cloves garlic, 2 pressed and 2 thinly sliced
- 2 lb. chicken wings
- 1/2 lb. shishito peppers
- 2 tbsp. plus 2 teaspoons canola oil
- Kosher salt
- 1 small red chile, thinly sliced
- Chopped cilantro and torn basil, for serving

Directions:

1. In large bowl, whisk together 2 tablespoons fish sauce, 1 tablespoon lime juice, and 1 tablespoon brown sugar to dissolve, then stir in pressed garlic and toss with wings. Refrigerate at least 1 hour and up to 3 hours.

2. Heat air fryer on 400°F. Transfer wings to air fryer (discard marinade), set timer to 15 minutes, press Start and cook 8 minutes.

3. Toss shishito peppers with 2 tsp oil and 1/4 teaspoon salt. Flip wings, scatter shishito peppers around wings, and continue cooking until wings are cooked through and peppers are browned in spots, 7 minutes more. Transfer to platter.

4. Meanwhile, in small skillet, heat remaining 2 tablespoons oil and sliced garlic on low, stirring, 4 minutes. Add chile and cook until garlic is golden brown and crisp, about 3 minutes more. Remove from heat and stir in remaining lime juice, fish sauce, and brown sugar. Spoon over wings and peppers and sprinkle with herbs

Air Fryer Shake And Bake Chicken

Servings: 4
Cooking Time: 18 Minutes

Ingredients:

- 4 boneless skinless chicken breasts about 6 ounces each
- 1/3 cup mayonnaise
- 1 shake and bake seasoning packet
- Homemade Shake and Bake Seasonings
- 1 cup Italian Seasoned Breadcrumbs
- 1 teaspoon salt
- 1 teaspoon paprika
- 1/2 teaspoon garlic powder
- 1/2 teaspoon ground black pepper

Directions:

1. Place chicken on cutting board or baking tray and pat dry with paper towels. Set aside.

2. Pour shake and bake packet or homemade coating into a brown paper bag or large storage bag.

3. Next lightly coat both sides of boneless chicken breasts with water, milk or oil so the coating will adhere to the chicken.

4. Place chicken into bag with seasonings. Seal or fold over top of bag and shake the chicken in coating mixture until each chicken piece is completely covered without any dry spots showing.

5. Prepare the air fryer basket by lightly spraying it with a nonstick cooking spray, line with air fryer parchment paper or use a perforated silicone mat. Place each piece of chicken into the basket in a

single layer and air fryer at 380 degrees F for 12-14 minutes, depending on the thickness.

6. Use a meat thermometer to make sure chicken is cooked through. Internal temperature for a chicken breast should be 165 degrees F. Thicker chicken breasts will require additional cooking time. Let chicken rest for a few minutes prior to serving.

NOTES

Substitute: Instead of water, milk or oil you can use an egg wash (lightly beaten egg) to brush chicken breasts which allows coating to also adhere.

Breadcrumbs method for dredging: For super crispy chicken pour all-purpose flour or coconut flour into a shallow bowl, next beat eggs in second bowl and last bread crumb mixture in third bowl. Dip each chicken piece in flour, egg and then breadcrumbs.

Lemon Za'atar Air Fryer Chicken

Ingredients:

- Whole chicken
- Olive oil
- Lemon zest + juice
- Za'atar. Za'atar is a spice blend made of oregano/marjoram, sumac and sesame seeds.
- Garlic. Garlic powder can be substituted
- Chilli flakes
- Salt and pepper

Directions:

1. Season the chicken: Mix the olive oil, lemon juice and zest, garlic and spices together. Transfer one third of the mixture to a separate bowl for basting. Brush the seasoned oil over the chicken, making sure to cover the entire chicken with the mix.

2. Cook in the Air Fryer: Preheat the air fryer to 160°C/320°F. Place the chicken, breast-side down, into the Air Fryer basket and cook for 20 mins. Flip over then brush with the reserved marinade. Cook for 10-20 minutes at 180°C/350°F. Check the doneness of the chicken after 10 minutes.

Depending on the size of your chicken, it might be cooked and won't need the full 10 minutes at 180. Turn the temperature up to 200°C/390°F and cook for another 5-10 minutes or until golden brown and crisp. Remove the chicken from the air fryer and allow to rest for 5-10 minutes then carve and serve.

Healthier Air Fryer Chicken Tacos

Servings: 4
Cooking Time: 20 Minutes

Ingredients:

- 1 1/2 cups panko breadcrumbs
- 35g sachet smokey chipotle seasoning
- 2 tsp finely grated lime rind
- 2 eggs
- 1/3 cup plain flour
- 500g chicken tenderloins
- 2 corn cobs, husks and silk removed, halved
- Olive oil spray
- 8 stand and stuff taco shells
- 80g mixed salad leaves
- Plain Greek-style yoghurt, to serve
- 2 tomatoes, diced
- 1 avocado, diced
- 1/4 cup fresh coriander leaves
- 1 tbsp lime juice, plus lime cheeks, to serve
- Select all ingredients

Directions:

1. To make salsa combine tomato, avocado, coriander and lime juice in a bowl. Season with salt and pepper. Cover. Refrigerate until required.

2. Meanwhile, combine breadcrumbs, seasoning and lime rind in a bowl. Season with salt and pepper. Whisk eggs in a separate shallow bowl. Place flour in another bowl. Toss chicken in flour, then dip in egg. Toss in breadcrumb mixture to coat evenly. Place on a plate. Spray chicken and corn with oil.

3. Place chicken and corn on racks in air fryer. Cook at 180°C for 12 minutes. Remove corn. Cook chicken for a further 5 to 8 minutes or until golden and cooked through. Transfer to a plate.
4. Place taco shells, upside-down on racks in air fryer. Cook at 180°C for 1 minute or until heated through.
5. Divide salad leaves among taco shells. Top with chicken, yoghurt and salsa. Serve with corn and lime cheeks.

Air Fryer Lemon Pepper Wings

Servings: 4
Cooking Time: 33 Minutes

Ingredients:
- 1 pound chicken wings
- 1 tablespoon olive oil
- 1 ½ tablespoons butter melted
- 1 ½ teaspoons lemon pepper seasoning

Directions:
1. Preheat air fryer to 400°F.
2. Dry wings and coat with olive oil and in a large bowl.
3. Place wings in a single layer in the basket and cook for 22 minutes flipping the wings after 10 minutes.
4. While the wings are cooking melt butter and combine in a bowl with the lemon pepper seasoning.
5. Remove wings from the air fryer and toss with the butter mixture.

Roasted Apple Cider Chicken With Potatoes & Onion

Ingredients:
- For the chicken marinade
- 3 lbs bone-in chicken thighs and legs
- ¾ cup apple cider
- ¼ cup olive oil
- 4 cloves garlic, minced
- 2 tsp paprika
- 1 tsp kosher salt
- 1 tsp onion powder
- ¼ tsp crushed rosemary
- ¼ tsp cracked black pepper
- 1/8 tsp allspice
- For the Potatoes and onions
- 1 ½ lbs baby potatoes, halved
- ½ yellow onion, cut into 1 inch pieces
- For the Apple cider glaze
- 1 cup apple cider
- 1 ½ Tbsp brown sugar
- 1 Tbsp sherry
- 1 tsp grainy mustard

Directions:
1. In a small bowl whisk together apple cider, olive oil, garlic, paprika, salt, onion powder, rosemary, pepper, and allspice. Add to a large Ziploc bag with chicken pieces, and toss to coat evenly. Allow to marinate for 30 min- 24 hours.
2. Place marinated chicken on a baking pan. Place parts skin side up and spread them evenly over the pan. Arrange the potatoes and onions around and under the chicken, filling in the spaces on the pan.
3. Bake at 400 F for 35 minutes or until the chicken is fully cooked and the potatoes are tender.
4. For the Cider Glaze
5. Add apple cider, brown sugar, sherry, and mustard to a small saucepan. Whisk and bring to a boil, then reduce heat to low. Summer mixture for 5-10 minutes, then turn off the heat. Let mixture sit, whisking occasionally, until thickened.
6. Remove baking dish from the oven. Pour the glaze over the chicken and potatoes. Garnish with chopper herbs.

Air Fryer Trader Joe's Frozen Kung Pao Chicken

Servings: 4
Cooking Time: 15 Minutes

Ingredients:

- 23 ounces (652g) Trader Joe's Frozen Kung Pao Chicken
- optional - chopped cilantro &/or green onion , for garnish
- oil spray , for the veggies
- EQUIPMENT
- Air Fryer

Directions:

1. Place the frozen orange chicken in the air fryer basket and spread out into a single even layer. No oil spray is needed. Set the sauce, vegetables, and peanuts aside (do not sauce the chicken yet).
2. Air Fry at 380°F/195°C for 8 minutes. Add the vegetables (if you like the peanuts toastier you can add them now too) and shake/stir to combine with the chicken pieces. Spray with oil spray to lightly coat the vegetables.
3. While the chicken and vegetables air fry: Warm the sauce in microwave or on stovetop until heated through.
4. Continue to Air Fry at 380°F/195°C for another 3-6 minutes or until heated through.
5. Toss cooked chicken with as much sauce as you like, peanuts, optional cilantro and/or green onion and serve.

Frozen Chicken Wings In Air Fryer

Servings: 4
Cooking Time: 25 Minutes

Ingredients:

- 12 chicken wings frozen
- 2 tsp Old Bay seasoning or your favorite blend of seasonings

Directions:

1. Allow wings to thaw for about 15 minutes. Prepare the air fryer basket with olive oil or nonstick spray.
2. Place frozen wings in a single layer into basket of the air fryer.
3. Cook wings at 400 degrees for 10 minutes.
4. Use a spatula or spoon to break them apart if needed, but they should be apart.
5. Add any seasonings to the wings and then air fry for an additional 16 minutes cook time, flipping the wings every 4 minutes until fully cooked and the skin is crispy and golden brown.
6. Use a meat thermometer to ensure the chicken is fully cooked before serving and add any additional time if needed.
7. Top with fresh parsley or dip into your favorite buffalo wing sauce or sauce of choice and serve with fresh celery or carrot sticks.

NOTES

I use a 5.8qt Cosori Air Fryer with this recipe. I find this recipe works perfectly with this brand of air fryer. If you're using a different manufacturer you may need to adjust the cooking time slightly to ensure you get perfectly crispy wings. All air fryer models are different and cook differently.

Frozen wings are typically already cut into pieces where the fresh wings are usually solid and have to be cut into pieces.

Before I get started, I allow the frozen wings to sit out of the freezer for about 15 minutes before cooking.

This air fryer recipe is one of my favorites because I can take the amount of frozen wings I want to cook and add them to the air fryer basket when ready.

Seasoning Frozen Air Fryer Chicken Wings is easy. After the first 10 minutes of cooking, the wings are generally detached and no longer frozen or stuck together.

Save leftover cooked wings in an airtight container and place them in the refrigerator for up to 3 days.

Air Fryer Popcorn Chicken

Servings: 4
Cooking Time: 10 Minutes

Ingredients:
- 1 tablespoon olive oil
- 1 ½ cup panko breadcrumbs*
- 1 teaspoon kosher salt (divided)
- 1 pound boneless (skinless chicken breasts)
- 2 tablespoons all-purpose flour
- 1 large egg
- 2 teaspoons garlic powder
- 2 teaspoons onion powder
- 1 teaspoon dried oregano
- 1/8 teaspoon cayenne pepper (optional)
- Freshly ground black pepper
- Olive oil spray
- Ketchup, Low Fat Ranch Dressing, BBQ Sauce, Honey Mustard, Marinara (Optional, for dipping)

Directions:
1. Add oil to a medium skillet over medium low heat. Add the panko and ½ teaspoon salt.
2. Toast panko for about 4 minutes or until just golden, stirring every 30 seconds to evenly brown. Transfer crumbs to a plate.
3. Cut chicken into ¾-inch cubes (about the size of a small dice), season with ¼ teaspoon salt and pepper, to taste, then set up your dredging station. You should have about 60 cubes.
4. To set up dredging station:
5. Place flour and ¼ teaspoon salt on a large plate.
6. Place egg in a bowl, add 1 teaspoon water and beat until uniform.
7. Add the garlic powder, onion powder, oregano and cayenne (if using) and black pepper, to taste, to the toasted panko and place the plate on the other side of the egg bowl.
8. Working with about 15 pieces at a time, dredge in flour, lightly coating all sides.
9. Then, egg, allowing excess to drip off (I like to use tongs and wipe the excess off on the side of the bowl). Next add the pieces to the panko mixture and coat all sides evenly, pressing crumbs to make sure they adhere evenly. Repeat with remaining pieces.
10. Preheat air fryer to 400 degrees F. Spray the basket with olive oil.
11. Add about 30 pieces to the air fryer basket, making sure to leave space between each piece so they get crispy. Spray the top with oil.
12. Cook for 5 minutes, shaking the basket halfway through cook time. Serve immediately.

NOTES

*1/4 cup breadcrumbs get thrown out

For best results, freeze Popcorn Chicken UNCOOKED.

Place chicken pieces in an even layer (not stacked top of each other) in a freezer safe container lined with parchment, adding a new piece of parchment to each layer.

When ready to cook, heat the air fryer to 400 degrees F. Spray the basket with oil then add 30 pieces, in an even layer. Cook for 8 minutes, shaking the basket halfway through cook time.

Breaded Chicken Cutlets With Deconstructed Guacamole

Servings: 4
Cooking Time: 20 Minutes

Ingredients:

- For The Chicken:
- 2 8 ounce boneless chicken breasts (cut in half lengthwise to make 4 thinner cutlets)
- 1/4 teaspoon seasoned salt (such as adobo seasoning)
- 2 large egg whites (beaten)
- 1/2 teaspoon Sazon (homemade or packaged)
- 1/2 cup seasoned breadcrumbs (or gluten-free crumbs)
- 1 -1/2 tbsp olive oil
- For the Deconstructed Guacamole:
- 4 ounces avocado (from 1 small Hass)
- 1 cup grape tomatoes (halved)
- 1/4 cup slivered red onion
- 1/4 cup cilantro leaves
- 1/4 teaspoon kosher salt and black pepper
- 1/4 teaspoon cumin
- juice of 1/2 lime
- 4 lime wedges for serving

Directions:

1. Season cutlets with seasoned salt. Place bread crumbs in a shallow bowl. In another bowl beat egg whites sazon together. Dip chicken cutlets in egg whites, then breadcrumb mixture, shaking off excess.
2. Heat a large nonstick frying pan on medium heat. Add the olive oil. When hot add the cutlets and cook about 6 minutes on each side, until golden brown and cooked through.
3. In a large bowl combine the avocado, red onion, tomato, cilantro, salt, pepper, cumin, and lime juice. Gently toss and serve over the chicken with additional lime wedges.
4. Air Fryer Directions:
5. Air fry in batches 400F 6 to 7 minutes turning halfway, until the crumbs are golden brown and the center is no longer pink.

Air Fryer Bbq Chicken Legs

Servings: 3
Cooking Time: 30 Minutes

Ingredients:

- 1 pound chicken legs (drumsticks or thighs-separated)
- 2 Tablespoons oil
- 2 Tablespoons BBQ sauce (or sugar-free bbq sauce for keto)
- 1 Tablespoon Worcestershire sauce
- 1/2 teaspoon salt , or to tase
- 1/4 teaspoon fresh crack black pepper , or to taste
- EQUIPMENT
- Air Fryer

Directions:

1. In bowl combine oil, bbq sauce, Worcestershire sauce, salt and pepper. Add chicken and stir to completely coat with in the marinade. Cover and marinate for about 20 minutes.
2. Pre-heat air fryer at 360°F/182°C for about 4 minutes. Spray the air fryer basket with oil or use an air fryer perforated parchment sheet. Place chicken in air fryer
3. Air Fry at 360°F/182°C for about 25-30 minutes, depending on the thickness of the drumsticks or thighs. Turn the chicken after cooking for 15 minutes.
4. Once cooked, let the chicken cool a bit and enjoy!

NOTES

Air Frying Tips and **NOTES**:

Shake or turn at least once while cooking. Don't overcrowd the air fryer basket.

If cooking in a non-preheated air fryer, it take longer to cook than if the Air Fryer is already pre-heated. Recipe timing is based on pre-heating the air fryer.

Recipes were tested in 3.4 to 6 qt air fryers. If using a larger air fryer, the recipe might cook quicker so adjust cooking time.

Remember to set a timer to shake/flip/toss as directed in recipe.

Air Fryer Chicken Thighs

Servings: 4
Cooking Time: 20 Minutes

Ingredients:

- 4-5 chicken thighs bone in, skin on
- 1 tbsp olive oil
- 1 tsp ground black pepper
- 1 tsp onion powder
- 1 tsp garlic powder

Directions:

1. Preheat the air fryer to 400 degrees Fahrenheit.
2. Rinse and pat the chicken thighs dry with a paper towel. Place the chicken in a small bowl and toss in the olive oil.
3. Add the seasonings to the chicken thighs and make sure to cover them evenly.
4. Place the thighs into the air fryer basket in a single layer.
5. Air Fry at 400 degrees Fahrenheit for 15 minutes of cooking time. Flip the chicken thighs and cook for an additional 8 minutes.
6. Use a meat thermometer to ensure the thighs have reached an internal temperature of 165 degrees Fahrenheit.
7. For a crispier skin, cook for an additional 1-2 minutes before serving.

NOTES

Serve this recipe with baked potatoes, biscuits, and gravy. Or, for a healthier meal, choose to serve them with a simple side salad with light dressing.

Weight Watchers 4 points
KETO C/2 P/19 F/22

Air Fryer Boneless Chicken Thighs

Servings: 4
Cooking Time: 20 Minutes

Ingredients:

- 4 chicken thighs
- ½ cup teriyaki sauce or any sauce
- 1 clove garlic minced
- ½ teaspoon sesame seeds

Directions:

1. Preheat air fryer 380°F.
2. Combine all ingredients in a medium bowl and mix until combined.
3. Place in the air fryer basket and cook for 17-20 minutes or until chicken reaches an internal temperature of 165°F.

NOTES

Pat chicken pieces dry with a clean paper towel before saucing so the sauce sticks before the pieces are added to the air fryer.

Always place the pieces in a single layer so the hot air can circulate around each piece making the outsides extra crispy.

Don't overcrowd the air fryer.

If using bone-in chicken, the cooking time will increase. The sauce will need to be added later in the cooking process so it doesn't burn.

FISH & SEAFOOD RECIPES

Air Fryer Shrimp Cocktail

Servings: 6
Cooking Time: 10 Minutes

Ingredients:

- FOR THE SHRIMP
- 1 pound (455 g) raw shrimp , deveined and shells removed
- 1 teaspoon (5 ml) oil , to coat shrimp
- salt , to taste
- black pepper , to taste
- SHRIMP COCKTAIL SAUCE
- 1/2 cup (120 g) ketchup (or low-carb tomato sauce for keto)
- 2 teaspoons (10 ml) Worcestershire sauce
- 1 teaspoon (5 ml) prepared horseradish
- 1 teaspoon (5 ml) fresh lemon juice
- 1/4 teaspoon (1.25 ml) celery salt
- 1/4 teaspoon (1.25 ml) garlic powder
- 1/4 teaspoon (1.25 ml) salt , or to taste
- black pepper to taste
- fresh lemon slices
- 1 (1) small cucumber , sliced (optional)
- fresh herbs for garnish (optional)
- EQUIPMENT
- Air Fryer

Directions:

1. In bowl, combine ketchup, Worcestershire sauce, horseradish, fresh lemon juice, celery salt, garlic powder, salt and black pepper. Stir until well mixed then set aside.
2. After shrimp shells are removed and de-veined, rinse and pat dry the shrimp. Coat shrimp with oil, and then season with salt and pepper. Place the shrimp in the air fryer basket or tray in a single layer.

3. Air Fry shrimp at 400°F for 8-12 minutes, or until cooked through. Shrimp comes in different sizes so check halfway through to make sure it's cooked enough or to your liking. After air frying, let the shrimp cool completely and chill in the fridge until ready to serve.
4. Serve the cooked shrimp with the shrimp cocktail sauce and slices of fresh lemon and cucumbers. Garnish with fresh herbs if you are feeling fancy.

Grain-free Tuna Cat Treats

Servings: 50
Cooking Time: 4 Hr

Ingredients:

- 1 can tuna, packed in water (5 ounces)
- 1 egg white
- Items Needed
- Food processor or blender
- Hand mixer
- Parchment paper
- Piping bag with small star nozzle attachment
- Parchment paper
- Piping bag with small star nozzle attachment

Directions:

1. Drain the canned tuna well and place the drained tuna in a food processor or blender. Set aside.
2. Place the egg white in a large mixing bowl. Using a hand mixer, beat the egg white until stiff peaks form.
3. Place 2 tablespoons of the whipped egg white in with the tuna. Blend thoroughly until the mixture is a smooth paste.
4. Remove the tuna paste mixture and gently fold into the remaining whipped egg white.
5. Transfer the mixture to a piping bag with a small star nozzle attachment.

6. Line the Food Dehydrator trays with parchment paper.
7. Pipe the mixture into small rounds on the parchment paper-lined trays.
8. Set temperature to 145°F and time to 4 hours, then press Start/Stop.
9. Remove the treats when done and crispy and crunchy. Cool completely, then serve to your pet.

Air Fryer Mahi Mahi

Servings: 2
Cooking Time: 10 Minutes

Ingredients:

- 2 mahi mahi filets
- 1/2 teaspoon paprika
- 1/2 teaspoon ground black pepper
- 1/2 teaspoon garlic powder
- 1 teaspoon olive oil

Directions:

1. In a small bowl combine paprika, ground black pepper and garlic powder. Set bowl aside.
2. Place fish fillets in a shallow dish and use a paper towel to pat fillets dry.
3. Use a pastry brush or spray the mahi mahi fillets with the cooking spray or olive oil.
4. Season mahi mahi with the mixture to completely coat in seasoning.
5. In a single layer place the fresh mahi mahi into the air fryer basket and cook at 400 degrees F / 200 C for 8-10 minutes.
6. Turning halfway through the cook time or until opaque and fish flakes. Use a fish spatula or kitchen tongs so each fillet stays together.
7. Serve fish hot once it's been removed from basket.

NOTES

I make this dish in my Cosori 5.8 qt. air fryer. Depending on your air fryer size and wattage cook time may need to be adjusted 1-2 minutes.

Optional Serving options: Spicy flavors, minced garlic, sweet paprika, squeeze of fresh lime juice or fresh lemon juice. Use fresh thyme, oregano, dill or parsley. Fajita seasoning, Cajun seasoning, taco seasoning, a chili powder mix or a pinch of salt, a pinch of bay seasoning, onion powder, or any bold spices your family enjoys. A family favorite fish seasoning will also be tasty.

Leftovers are great as fish tacos on a corn tortilla with corn salsa.

Teriyaki-glazed Salmon

Servings: 4

Ingredients:

- 1 1/2 lb. salmon fillet
- Kosher salt and pepper
- 1/2 c. Honey-Lime Teriyaki Sauce, divided
- 1/4 c. rice vinegar
- 1 tsp. honey
- 1/2 tsp. grated peeled fresh ginger
- 1 shallot, thinly sliced
- 2 Persian cucumbers, thinly sliced
- Cilantro, for sprinkling

Directions:

1. Heat oven to 400°F. Place salmon on foil-lined baking sheet, season with 1/4 teaspoon salt, then spoon 3 tablespoons teriyaki sauce on top and roast 10 minutes. Spoon remaining teriyaki sauce over top and continue roasting 8 minutes.
2. Increase heat to broil. Baste salmon with any sauce that has fallen to sides of pan and broil until sticky and opaque throughout, 2 to 4 minutes.
3. Meanwhile, in bowl, whisk together vinegar, honey, and 1/4 teaspoon each salt and pepper to dissolve. Stir in ginger then shallot and let sit 5 minutes. Add cucumber and let sit, tossing occasionally, 10 minutes. Transfer salmon to platter and, with slotted spoon, spoon cucumber mixture over top and sprinkle with cilantro.
4. AIR FRYER DIRECTIONS:
5. Remove the insert from air-fryer basket. Heat air-fryer to 400°F. Place a sheet of aluminum foil on

top of the insert and place salmon on top of that. Season with 1/4 teaspoon salt. Drizzle with 2 tablespoons teriyaki sauce. Return the insert (with the salmon) to air-fryer basket and air-fry, basting every 5 minutes with any sauce that has fallen to sides of salmon (and additional sauce if necessary), until opaque throughout and sticky on top, 15 to 18 minutes.

Air Fryer Tuna Melts

Ingredients:

- 12 oz tuna
- 2 dil pickles
- 1/4 medium onion
- 1/4 cup mayonnaise
- Garlic Powder
- Black Pepper
- Bread of choice
- 4 slices of american cheese

Directions:

1. In a large bowl mix together your tuna, pickles, onion, mayonnaise, garlic powder, and black pepper.
2. Top 4 of the slices of bread with the tuna mixture and add a slice of cheese to each.
3. Toast at 400 degrees for 5 minutes
4. Carefully remove from the air fryer and enjoy!

Air Fryer Crab Rangoon

Servings: 7
Cooking Time: 10 Minutes

Ingredients:

- 5 ounces cream cheese
- 5 ounces crab meat
- 2 green onions, chopped
- 1 teaspoons worcestershire
- 1 1/2 teaspoons minced garlic
- salt and pepper to taste
- olive oil cooking spray
- 28 wonton wrappers
- water

Directions:

1. In a medium bowl, combine the cream cheese, crab meat, green onions, worcestershire, minced garlic and salt and pepper.
2. Place one wonton wrapper on a cutting board. Use a brush to brush the edges of the wrapper with water.
3. Fill the center of the wrapper with 1 ½ teaspoons of crab mixture.
4. Grab two opposite corners of the wrapper to come together in the middle to make a triangle. Then take the other ends and bring them to the middle as well. Press to make sure you get all the air out and seal the seams together.
5. Spray the bottom of your air fryer. Then place your crab rangoons in the basket. Spritz the tops of the rangoons with a little more cooking spray.
6. Bake at 360 for 10 minutes, Checking at the 5 minute mark and then every 2 minutes after, to check on how brown and crispy you want them. Depending on your air fryer brand and size, cooking time varies slightly. Serve with sweet chili sauce.

Air Fryer Fish And Chips

Servings: 4
Cooking Time: 12 Minutes

Ingredients:

- 3/4 cup all purpose flour
- 2 teaspoons smoked paprika
- 1/2 teaspoon garlic powder
- 1/2 teaspoon sea salt
- 1/2 teaspoon ground black pepper
- 1 large egg
- 1/2 cup panko breadcrumbs
- 1 pound cod filet, cut into strips
- 1/2 teaspoon olive oil spray

Directions:

1. First set up your dredging stations.

2. In a small bowl mix the flour with paprika, garlic powder, sea salt and ground black pepper together.

3. In a separate bowl whisk the egg and a spoonful of cold water to create an egg wash.

4. Place the panko breadcrumbs in a third shallow bowl.

5. Lay the fish strips on a cutting board and pat dry with a paper towel.

6. Dredge the fish in the flour mixture and shake off the excess flour, then dip in egg mixture and lastly into the breadcrumb mixture, pressing down lightly so the breadcrumbs adhere to the fish (shake off any excess batter).

7. Place each fillet on a baking sheet until dredging all the fish is complete.

8. Spray both sides of the seasoned fish fillets with cooking spray.

9. Place the cod fish strips into the air fryer basket in a single layer, be sure not to overcrowd.

10. Air fry at 400 degrees F for 10-12 minutes, flipping the fish halfway through the cooking process, until they are crispy and golden brown.

11. Use a fork to check for desired doneness, it should flake easily (internal temperature should be 145 degrees F). Cooking times may need to be an additional couple of minutes, depending on the thickness of the fish.

12. When cooking fish in batches, place first batch on a cooking rack so they remain crispy.

13. So once the fish are done cooking, prepare the air fryer to make russet potato chips.

14. Serve together while hot.

NOTES

Optional Favorite Dipping Sauce: Tartar sauce, lemon wedges, sweet chili sauce, ketchup or lemon slices with malt vinegar.

Cooking Tips: Place a piece of parchment paper in air fryer basket this will ensure fish does not stick and make for easier clean up.

Substitutions: Use tapioca flour, almond flour, cassava flour, gluten-free flour and coconut flour in place of all-purpose flour.

I make this recipe in my Cosori 5.8 qt. air fryer. Depending on your air fryer, size and wattages, cook time may need to be adjusted 1-2 minutes.

Air Fryer Salmon Flatbreads

Servings: 4

Ingredients:

- 1 tbsp. red wine vinegar
- 2 tbsp. olive oil, divided
- 1 tbsp. capers, chopped
- 2 scallions, 1 finely chopped and 1 thinly sliced
- Kosher salt and pepper
- 1 pt. grape tomatoes
- 1 lb. skinless salmon filet, cut into 11/2 inch pieces
- 1 tbsp. chopped flat-leaf parsley
- Labneh or Greek yogurt, for serving
- 4 pieces naan or flatbread, warmed
- 2 c. baby arugula or kale
- Sliced scallion, for serving
- Crumbled feta, for serving

Directions:

1. In small bowl, combine red wine vinegar, 1 tablespoon olive oil, capers, chopped scallion, and 1/4 teaspoon pepper; set aside.

2. Heat air fryer to 400°F. In bowl, toss tomatoes and remaining tablespoon oil with 1/4 teaspoon each salt and pepper. Season salmon with 1/4 teaspoon each salt and pepper.

3. Place salmon in single layer on 1 side of air fryer and add tomatoes to remaining space (piling them is great). Air-fry until salmon is just barely opaque throughout, 6 minutes.

4. Transfer tomatoes to bowl with vinegar-scallion mix and toss to combine, then toss with parsley.

5. Spread labneh or yogurt on flatbreads, top with salmon and arugula, then spoon tomato mixture on top. Sprinkle with sliced scallions and crumbled feta if desired.

Air Fryer Lobster Tails With Lemon-garlic Butter

Servings: 2
Cooking Time: 10 Minutes

Ingredients:

- 2 (4 ounce) lobster tails
- 4 tablespoons butter
- 1 teaspoon lemon zest
- 1 clove garlic, grated
- salt and ground black pepper to taste
- 1 teaspoon chopped fresh parsley
- 2 wedges lemon

Directions:

1. Preheat an air fryer to 380 degrees F (195 degrees C).
2. Butterfly lobster tails by cutting lengthwise through the centers of the hard top shells and meat with kitchen shears. Cut to, but not through, the bottoms of the shells. Spread tail halves apart. Place tails in the air fryer basket with lobster meat facing up.
3. Melt butter in a small saucepan over medium heat. Add lemon zest and garlic; heat until garlic is fragrant, about 30 seconds.
4. Transfer 2 tablespoons of butter mixture to a small bowl; brush this onto lobster tails. Discard any remaining brushed butter to avoid contamination from uncooked lobster. Season lobster with salt and pepper.
5. Cook in the preheated air fryer until lobster meat is opaque, 5 to 7 minutes.
6. Spoon reserved butter from the saucepan over lobster meat. Top with parsley and serve with lemon wedges.
7. Tips
8. You can use frozen lobster tails, just thaw them first before proceeding with instructions.
9.

Dorito-crumbed Fillets

Servings: 4

Ingredients:

- 4 Vegetarian Quorn Fillets
- 150ml buttermilk (or sub for 130ml/4.55fl. oz milk + 1 tbsp apple cider vinegar)
- 90g tangy cheese tortilla chips (1/2 a sharing bag)
- 1 egg
- 30g plain flour
- Salt & pepper
- To serve salsa
- COOKING MODE
- When entering cooking mode - We will enable your screen to stay 'always on' to avoid any unnecessary interruptions whilst you cook!

Directions:

1. Place the Quorn Fillets in a large bowl. Cover with buttermilk. Cover and place in the fridge for 4 hours or overnight to marinate
2. Preheat one zone of your Ninja Foodi Dual Zone Air Fryer to 180°C. Line a baking tray with baking paper
3. Place the tortilla chips in a food processor and pulse until coarsely chopped. Transfer to a plate
4. Crack the egg into a shallow bowl and whisk. Place the flour, a pinch of salt & pepper on a separate plate and mix
5. Drain the Quorn, discarding the buttermilk. Place the Quorn on the flour and roll a few times to coat. Dip in the egg, then in tortilla chips, pressing firmly to coat. Transfer to the prepared tray
6. Place the fillets in the air fryer, select Air Fry, and set time to 10 minutes, Select Start/Stop and fry until golden and cooked through
7. Transfer to a serving platter. Serve with salsa & Mexican style rice

Air Fryer Catfish

Servings: 4
Cooking Time: 22 Minutes

Ingredients:

- 1 pound catfish fillets
- 1 cup fish fry breading I prefer Louisiana brand
- 1 small lemon cut into wedges
- 1 Tablespoon olive oil

Directions:

1. Preheat the Air Fryer to 400 degrees Fahrenheit for 5 minutes.
2. Rinse and dry the catfish with a paper towel before coating.
3. Add the seasoned breading to a shallow bowl and then dip each piece of fish until coated completely. Spray the sides of each fillet with olive oil spray.
4. Place fillets in the prepared Air Fryer basket in a single layer. Cook at 400°F for 10 minutes, then carefully flip the catfish filets and cook for an additional 10 minutes.
5. Flip once more and cook for an additional 1-2 minutes to get them extra crispy if desired.
6. Serve with coleslaw and tartar sauce. Squeeze fresh lemon juice over the filets just before serving.

NOTES

NOTE: This recipe was made using a 1700 watt 5.8 qt Basket style Cosori Air Fryer. Your brand of air fryer may cook differently depending on the size and the power of the air fryer. Use this recipe as a guide when using a different brand of air fryer.

Laying a piece of parchment paper in the Air Fryer makes cleaning up super easy. After cooking, all you have to do is remove the parchment paper from the Air Fryer! There's no greasy residue left, making cleaning up super quick and painless!

To ensure your fish has a crunchy crust, make sure you tap some of the excess breading off, so the fish isn't too bready. In addition, Use spray oil instead of olive oil, so the fish isn't too soggy.

New England Baked Cod

Ingredients:

- 2 fillets cod
- 1 cup butter-flavored crackers
- 2 Tbsp parsley, minced
- 1 Tbsp Parmesan, grated
- 1 tsp Auntie NoNo's Everything Seasoning
- 1 Tbsp lemon juice
- 1 Tbsp lemon zest
- 3 Tbsp unsalted butter, melted

Directions:

1. In a bowl, mix together the crackers, parsley, Parmesan, Auntie NoNo's Everything Seasoning, lemon juice and zest to make the topping.
2. Add in half of the melted butter.
3. Pat dry the cod fillets and spread on the remaining melted butter.
4. Season the cod to taste. We used some more Auntie NoNo's Everything Seasoning.
5. Spoon on the cracker mixture on top of the fish and press down as best as possible. Some of the mixture will fall off, but just do your best to get as much on the top.
6. Transfer the fish to the air fryer basket.
7. Air fry at 350°F for about 13 minutes, or until your fish reaches an internal temperature of 145°F.
8. Finish them off with some more lemon juice and enjoy!!

Lemon-pepper Air-fryer Shrimp And Veggies

Servings: 2

Ingredients:

- 10 ounce fresh or frozen extra-large shrimp in shells, thawed if frozen, peeled, and deveined
- 2 lemons
- 1 tablespoon olive oil
- 1 teaspoon salt-free lemon-pepper seasoning, such as Mrs. Dash

- ¼ teaspoon salt
- ¼ teaspoon garlic powder
- ¼ teaspoon paprika
- 1 small zucchini, halved lengthwise and sliced 1/4 inch thick
- 2 medium carrots, sliced

Directions:

1. Thaw shrimp if frozen. Rinse shrimp; pat dry. Preheat air fryer at 400°F.
2. Squeeze 3 Tbsp. juice from one of the lemons; cut the remaining lemon into wedges. In a large bowl combine lemon juice and the next five ingredients (through paprika). Add shrimp, zucchini, and carrots; toss to coat.
3. Using a slotted spoon, transfer shrimp mixture to air-fryer basket. Cook 9 to 11 minutes or until shrimp are opaque, stirring occasionally. Serve with lemon wedges.

Frozen Cod In The Air Fryer

Servings: 2
Cooking Time: 14 Minutes

Ingredients:

- 2 frozen cod loin filets
- 1-2 tablespoons olive oil
- BLACKENING SEASONING
- 1 tablespoon paprika
- 2 teaspoons garlic powder
- 2 teaspoons onion powder
- 1 teaspoon kosher salt
- 1 teaspoon black pepper
- ½ teaspoon cayenne pepper
- ½ teaspoon dried oregano
- ½ teaspoon dried thyme
- FOR SERVING
- Lemon wedges

Directions:

1. In a small bowl, combine blackening seasoning ingredients and whisk well.

2. Rub oil on the frozen fish, then rub 2-3 tablespoons of the seasoning on immediately. Store additional seasoning in a small container for future use.
3. Place the cod pieces in a single layer in the basket.
4. Air fry at 350 degrees F for 4 minutes. Turn the heat up to 370 degrees F and air fry for 8-10 minutes. Flip the fish and air fry for 2-4 additional minutes until the fish is fully cooked and opaque.

Bang Bang Shrimp

Servings: 4
Cooking Time: 6 Minutes

Ingredients:

- 1 lb shrimp shells and tails removed
- 1 tablespoon lemon juice
- 1 cup heavy cream
- 1/2 cup almond flour
- 1/2 cup keto bread crumbs
- 1/2 teaspoon salt
- 1/2 teaspoon pepper
- 1/4 cup oil to fry
- For the bang bang sauce
- 1/2 cup mayonnaise
- 2 tablespoons sriracha
- 2 tablespoons keto honey
- 1 teaspoon vinegar

Directions:

1. Whisk together the lemon juice and heavy cream in a small bowl and let it sit for 5 minutes.
2. In a small bowl, add the bang bang sauce ingredients and whisk together until smooth.
3. In a mixing bowl, whisk together the almond flour, keto bread crumbs, salt, and pepper.
4. Bread the shrimp by coating it in the breading, then the buttermilk, then back in the breading. Repeat until all the shrimp are breaded.
5. Add the oil into a non-stick pan and place it over medium heat. Once hot, add the shrimp and cook for 3-4 minutes, flipping halfway through. Repeat the process until all the shrimp is cooked.

6. Toss the fried shrimp with the sauce and serve immediately.

NOTES

TO STORE: Leftover shrimp can be stored in the refrigerator, covered, for up to three days. The sauce will keep longer, closer to one week.

TO FREEZE: Place the cooked and cooled shrimp in an airtight container and store it in the freezer for up to two months.

TO REHEAT: Add the shrimp to a non-stick pan and heat until the shrimp is hot.

Cornflake Crusted Salmon And Lemon Cardamom Veg

Servings: 4

Ingredients:

- For the lemon cardamom veg
- 75g almonds
- 2 tbsp coconut oil
- 3 cloves garlic (peeled, finely chopped)
- 6 Seeds of cardamom pods
- 3/4 tsp sea salt
- 1 medium head of broccoli (approx. 350g, cut into florets)
- 200g shredded cavolo nero
- 1 Zest and juice of lemon
- For the cornflake crusted salmon
- 4 salmon fillets (roughly 130g each)
- 4 tbsp mayonnaise
- 2 tbsp whole grain mustard
- 1/4 tsp garlic granules
- 1/4 tsp onion granules
- Pinch sea salt
- 100g gluten-free cornflakes
- Cooking spray
- COOKING MODE
- When entering cooking mode - We will enable your screen to stay 'always on' to avoid any unnecessary interruptions whilst you cook!

Directions:

1. Add the almonds to zone 1 drawer, without the crisper plate installed. Select Zone 1, then turn the dial to AIR FRY and set the temperature to 180°C and the time to 6 minutes. Press START/STOP to begin cooking. Shake the almonds halfway through cooking then transfer to a plate and leave to cool down before roughly chopping.

2. In a small bowl stir together the mayonnaise, mustard, garlic granules, onion granules and sea salt until combined. Divide equally between the salmon fillets, spreading over the tops and sides.

3. Crush the gluten-free cornflakes by hand or place them into a ziplock bag and bash with a rolling pin until you get a coarse crumb. Spoon over the salmon fillets and gently pat until coated evenly.

4. Insert the crisper plate into the zone 2 drawer and spray with cooking spray. Place the salmon fillets into the drawer and close.

5. Add the coconut oil, chopped garlic, and cardamom seeds to the zone 1 drawer and close. Select Zone 1, then turn the dial to AIR FRY and set the temperature to 180°C and the time to 8 minutes. Press MATCH, then START/STOP to begin cooking.

6. After 1 minute add the sea salt and broccoli florets to the zone 1 drawer, shake or stir, then close the drawer and cook for 5 minutes before adding the shredded cavolo nero.

7. When the unit has finished cooking add the chopped toasted almonds, lemon juice and zest to the zone 1 and stir. Serve the salmon and vegetables immediately and enjoy.

Fish Fingers With Coleslaw

Servings: 4
Cooking Time: 25 Minutes

Ingredients:

- Fish fingers with coleslaw
- 1 kilogram white fish fillets, skin and bones removed, coarsely chopped
- 2 tablespoon coarsely chopped fresh chives
- 2 egg whites
- 1 1/4 cup (125 grams) packaged breadcrumbs
- 2 tablespoon olive oil
- Coleslaw
- 1 1/2 cup (120 grams) finely shredded red cabbage
- 1 cup (80 grams) finely shredded savoy cabbage
- 1 medium carrot, coarsely grated
- 2 tablespoon coarsely chopped fresh flat-leaf parsley
- 1 green onion, thinly sliced
- 2 tablespoon mayonnaise
- 1 tablespoon sour cream
- 1 tablespoon white wine vinegar

Directions:

1. Fish fingers with coleslaw
2. Make coleslaw.
3. Grease 20cm x 30cm rectangular pan.
4. Blend or process fish and chives until smooth. Press mixture evenly into pan, turn out onto a baking-paper-lined tray; cut into eight 20cm slices; cut each slice in half to make 16 fish fingers.
5. In a medium shallow bow whisk egg whites lightly; in another medium shallow bowl, place breadcrumbs. Dip fish fingers into egg whites, then in breadcrumbs to coat. In a large frying pan, heat oil over medium-high heat; cook fish fingers, in batches, 3 minutes or until browned lightly and cooked through. Drain on absorbent paper. Cut fish fingers into bite-sized pieces for toddlers.
6. Serve fish fingers with coleslaw; season to taste.
7. Coleslaw
8. In a large bowl, combine ingredients.

Air Fryer Bacon Wrapped Scallops

Servings: 4
Cooking Time: 20 Minutes

Ingredients:

- 16 large sea scallops (cleaned and pat dry with paper towels)
- 8 slices center cut bacon
- 16 toothpicks
- olive oil spray
- freshly ground black pepper (to taste)

Directions:

1. Preheat air fryer to 400F 3 minutes.
2. Place the bacon in the air fryer to partially cook 3 minutes, turning halfway. Remove and set on a paper towel to cool.
3. Remove any side muscles on the scallops. Pat the scallops dry with paper towels to remove any moisture.
4. Wrap each scallop in slice of bacon and secure it with a toothpick.
5. Spritz olive oil over scallops and season lightly with black pepper.
6. Arrange scallops in a single layer in the air fryer, cook, in batches 8 minutes turning halfway until scallop is tender and opaque and bacon is cooked through. Serve hot.

Air Fried Salmon

Ingredients:

- Salmon (your choice on the size)
- 1/2 tsp. smoked paprika
- 1/2 tsp. garlic powder
- 1/2 tsp. salt

Directions:

1. Slice salmon into even slices
2. Place sliced salmon into the air fryer and use a brush to oil both sides
3. Sprinkle seasoning onto the salmon
4. Close air fryer and set the temperature to 400F and time to 8 minutes. Technically you can set the time from 8-10 minutes
5. Enjoy!

Lemon & Garlic Air Fryer Scallops

Servings: 2
Cooking Time: 10 Minutes

Ingredients:

- 8 large scallops, shelled, fresh
- 5ml olive oil spray
- 2 tbs olive oil
- 1 clove garlic, peeled and minced
- For the dressing
- 20g capers, drained and chopped
- 2 medium lemons, 1 juiced and zested, 1 chopped into wedges
- 2 tbs parsley, fresh, chopped

Directions:

1. Spray the air fryer basket with olive oil spray and add the scallops, leaving space between each. Spray with more oil and cook at 200°C for 5-6 minutes, depending on the size of the scallops.
2. Whisk the oil, garlic, lemon juice and zest and parsley together. Serve the scallops drizzled with dressing with lemon wedges on the side

Air Fryer Garlic Shrimp With Lemon

Servings: 2-3
Cooking Time: 15 Minutes

Ingredients:

- 1 pound (454 g) raw shrimp , peeled de-veined,
- Vegetable oil or spray , to coat shrimp
- 1/4 teaspoon (1.25 ml) garlic powder
- Salt , to taste
- Black pepper , to taste
- lemon wedges
- minced parsley and/or chili flakes (optional)
- EQUIPMENT
- Air Fryer

Directions:

1. In a bowl add the shrimp, garlic powder, salt and pepper and toss to coat all of the shrimp evenly. Add shrimp to air fryer basket in a single layer.
2. Air fry at 400°F for about 8-14 minutes (depending on the size of your shrimp), gently shaking and flipping halfway.
3. Add the cooked shrimp to bowl, squeeze lemon juice on top. Sprinkle parsley and/or chili flakes and serve hot. So good!

Air Fryer Frozen Fish Sticks

Servings: 4
Cooking Time: 10 Minutes

Ingredients:

- 1 box Frozen Fish Sticks
- Optional: Dipping Sauces

Directions:

1. Make delicious and crispy fish sticks, begin with grabbing a box of your favorite frozen food brand of breaded fish sticks.
2. To prevent the fish sticks from sticking, lightly brush or spray with oil. Place the fish fingers in a

single layer in the air fryer tray, or air fryer basket. Work in batches to avoid overlap in the basket.

3. Air Fry at 400 degrees Fahrenheit for 10-12 minutes cook time, at the 5 minute mark flip them over during the cooking process.

4. Once the outside is golden brown and crispy, remove fish sticks from basket. Serve with your favorite dipping sauce.

NOTES

I would not suggest doing more than one layer of fish sticks while air frying or they may not cook as evenly or be as crispy as you would like them to be.

Air fryer times may vary depending on the wattage and air fryer model. Additional cook times may need to be adjusted by 2-4 minutes.

Salmon Quiche

Servings: 6

Ingredients:

- All-purpose flour, as needed, for dusting
- 1 store-bought (9-inch / 22-centimeter diameter) pre-made pie crust
- Floured baking spray
- Dry beans, for blind baking the crust
- 3 large eggs
- 1 cup (236 milliliters) heavy cream
- 2 teaspoons (10 grams) ground nutmeg
- 2 teaspoons (10 grams) smoked paprika
- 2 teaspoons (10 grams) kosher salt
- 1 teaspoon ground black pepper
- ½ cup (55 grams) gruyere cheese, shredded
- ¼ cup (22 grams) Parmesan cheese, shredded
- 1 cup (30 grams) baby spinach, rough chopped
- 10 ounces (283 grams) skin off salmon, cut into 1-inch (2½-centimeter) pieces
- Items Needed:
- Parchment paper
- 8-inch (20-centimeter) cake pan or tart pan

Directions:

1. Roll out the pie crust on a flat clean surface, lightly dusted with some flour. Make sure the entire crust is evenly flat and smooth, and at least ¼-inch thick.

2. Spray the cake pan with floured baking spray and gently place the dough on top.

3. Press the dough gently down into the pan and trim off excess, leaving at least ½-inch of dough above the cake pan.

4. Dock the pie crust by pressing holes into the crust with a fork across the entire crust surface.

5. Place a sheet of parchment paper on top of the crust and fill the entire cake pan with dried beans. Trim off excess parchment paper, leaving at least a ½-inch paper rim.

6. Place the pie crust directly into the Smart Air Fryer basket, without the crisper plate.

7. Select the Bake function, adjust temperature to 400°F and time to 10 minutes, then press Start/Pause.

8. Remove the pie crust when done, let it cool completely, and then remove the beans and parchment paper.

9. Combine the eggs, heavy cream, nutmeg, paprika, salt, black pepper, both cheeses, and spinach in a medium bowl. Add in the salmon and mix well.

10. Pour the egg mixture into the cooled pie crust. Then place the cake pan into the air fryer basket.

11. Select the Bake function, adjust temperature to 345°F and time to 20 minutes, then press Start/Pause.

12. Pause the air fryer when there are 5 minutes remaining and carefully cover the quiche with foil and resume cooking.

13. Remove the quiche when done and allow it to cool completely before slicing and serving.

14. Note: To remove the entire quiche from the cake pan, cool for 30 minutes in the fridge, then run a butter knife along the edge of the cake pan and crust.

Air Fryer Fried Shrimp

Servings: 4
Cooking Time: 12-18 Minutes

Ingredients:

- 1 pound uncooked large shrimp (26 to 30 per pound), thawed if frozen
- 1/2 cup all-purpose flour
- 1 teaspoon seasoning salt, such as Lawry's
- 2 large eggs
- 1 1/2 cups panko breadcrumbs
- Cooking spray

Directions:

1. Peel and devein 1 pound large shrimp, if needed, and set aside.
2. Combine 1/2 cup all-purpose flour and 1 teaspoon seasoning salt in a shallow dish or bowl. Lightly beat 2 large eggs in a second bowl. Place 1 1/2 cups panko bread crumbs in a third bowl.
3. Heat an air fryer to 400°F. Working in batches of enough shrimp to sit in the air fryer basket with plenty of space around each one, coat the shrimp: coat first in the flour mixture, then dip in the egg. Let the excess egg drip back into the bowl, then coat the shrimp completely in the panko. Place on a plate.
4. Coat with cooking spray. Arrange the shrimp in the air fryer with plenty of space around each one to ensure they air fry instead of steaming. Air fry until golden brown, about 6 minutes. Transfer to a serving plate and repeat coating and air-frying the remaining shrimp.

NOTES

Recipe **NOTES**: If you overcrowd the basket, the shrimp will steam rather than fry and won't be as crispy. Cook in batches, and the second batch may cook faster.
Storage: Leftovers can be refrigerated in an airtight container up to 2 days.

Air Fryer Coconut Shrimp

Servings: 4
Cooking Time: 10 Minutes

Ingredients:

- 1 lb large shrimp peeled
- 2 large eggs
- 1 cup unsweetened coconut flakes
- 1/2 cup panko bread crumbs
- 1/2 cup all-purpose flour
- 1/2 teaspoon garlic powder
- 1/2 teaspoon smoked paprika
- 1/2 teaspoon salt
- 1/2 teaspoon pepper

Directions:

1. Preheat the air fryer to 180C/350F.
2. In a bowl, beat the eggs. In a separate bowl, combine the coconut flakes with the bread crumbs. In a third bowl, add the flour, smoked paprika, salt, pepper, and garlic powder.
3. Dip the shrimp in the flour, shake off excess, then the egg mixture, and then in the coconut and panko mixture, pressing firmly for it to stick. Repeat the process.
4. Grease the air fryer basket, then add the coconut shrimp to it, ensuring that they are not touching one another.
5. Air fry for 10-12 minutes, flipping halfway through.
6. Once the shrimp are golden brown, remove them from the air fryer basket and serve immediately.

NOTES

TO STORE: Keep the air fried coconut shrimp in an airtight container in the fridge for up to 3 days.
TO FREEZE: Once they're cooked and cooled to room temperature, place them in an airtight container and freeze for up to 2 months.
TO REHEAT: Place the chilled or frozen coconut shrimp in the air fryer and reheat until warmed through.

Air Fryer Honey Mustard Salmon

Cooking Time: 12 Minutes

Ingredients:

- 2-4 portions Salmon 4-6 ounces each
- 1 tablespoon olive oil
- 1/2 teaspoon salt
- 1/2 teaspoon pepper
- 2 tablespoon Dijon Mustard
- 2 tablespoon Honey

Directions:

1. Lightly brush or spray the bottom of the basket with olive oil.
2. Place salmon portions in the basket and season with salt and pepper to your preference.
3. In a small bowl, stir the honey and Dijon mustard together.
4. Use a brush or a spoon, and evenly coat the tops of each salmon portion with the honey mustard mixture.
5. Close the basket and cook at 380 degrees Fahrenheit for 10-12 minutes.
6. Check for doneness using a fork. Serve immediately.

NOTES

Weight Watchers: Approx 3-5 points

Air Fryer Scallops

Servings: 4
Cooking Time: 5 Minutes

Ingredients:

- 1 pound scallops
- 1 tablespoon olive oil
- 1 teaspoon cajun seasoning

Directions:

1. Preheat air fryer to 400°F.
2. Remove scallops from the packaging and pat dry with a paper towel.
3. Combine seasoning, oil, and scallops in a bowl and toss to combine.
4. Place scallops in the air fryer basket and cook for 5-6 minutes.

Air Fryer Shrimp Tempura

Servings: 4
Cooking Time: 30 Minutes

Ingredients:

- 1 pound fresh jumbo shrimp
- 1 ¼ cups all-purpose flour, divided
- ½ cup cold water
- 2 egg whites (or 1 large egg), beaten
- ⅓ cup cornstarch
- ½ teaspoon salt

Directions:

1. Prepare the shrimp by deveining them (if necessary) and removing the shell up to the tail. Make 4-5 small notches on the "belly" of each shrimp and stretch them out. Pat them dry with paper towels.
2. In a bowl, whisk together ½ cup of the flour, water, and egg whites. In a second bowl, add the remaining flour.
3. Place cornstarch and salt in a plastic zipper bag. Add shrimp and toss well to coat.
4. Preheat the air fryer to 370 degrees F for 5 minutes. Spray the inner basket generously with cooking oil spray.
5. Dip shrimp, one at a time, in the wet flour batter, then dredge them through the dry flour to lightly coat them. Place them on a clean plate or parchment-lined baking sheet.
6. Working in batches, set the shrimp in the basket in a single, uncrowded layer. Spray them well with cooking oil spray, then air fry for 7-8 minutes, until lightly golden.
7. FROM FROZEN:
8. Prep shrimp through step 5, then place the plate or baking sheet in the freezer for 1 hour to flash-freeze.

Remove the shrimp and store in a plastic zipper bag until ready to cook.

9. When ready to cook, preheat the air fryer to 370 degrees F for 5 minutes. Spray the inner basket with cooking oil spray.

10. Working in batches, set the frozen shrimp in the basket in a single, uncrowded layer. Spray them well with cooking oil spray, then air fry for 12-15 minutes, until lightly golden.

NOTES

HOW TO REHEAT SHRIMP TEMPURA:

Preheat your air fryer to 370 degrees.

Place shrimp in air fryer basket and cook for 3-5 minutes or until hot.

Chipotle Tuna Melt

Ingredients:

- 1 can (5 ounces) tuna
- 3 tablespoons La Costeña Chipotle Sauce
- 4 slices white bread
- 2 slices pepper jack cheese

Directions:

1. SELECT Preheat on the Air Fryer, adjust to 320°F, and press Start/Pause.

2. MIX the tuna and chipotle sauce until combined.

3. SPREAD half of the chipotle tuna mixture onto each of 2 bread slices.

4. ADD a slice of pepper jack cheese onto each and top with the remaining 2 bread slices, making 2 sandwiches.

5. PLACE the sandwiches into the preheated air fryer.

6. SELECT Bread, adjust time to 8 minutes, and press Start/Pause.

7. CUT diagonally and serve.

Seafood Paella

Servings: 3-4
Cooking Time: 1 Hr

Ingredients:

- 2 teaspoons extra-virgin olive oil
- ½ tablespoon garlic, minced
- ½ yellow onion, small diced
- 1 teaspoon kosher salt, plus more to taste
- ¼ teaspoon saffron or ½ teaspoon turmeric
- 1 teaspoon paprika
- ½ cup tomatoes, diced
- 1 cup plus 2 tablespoons chicken broth
- 2 bay leaves
- 1 cup medium grain white rice, rinsed and drained
- ½ cup frozen green peas
- 7 large shrimps (31/35 size), peeled and deveined
- 8 clams
- 7 mussels
- Parsley, chopped, for garnish
- 1 lemon, sliced into wedges, for serving
- Items Needed
- Small stock pot with lid

Directions:

1. Set Mode to Sauté on the Rice Cooker, adjust time to 20 minutes, then tap Start.

2. Add the oil to the pot, then add the garlic and onions and cook until aromatic.

3. Add the salt, saffron or turmeric, paprika, tomatoes, and chicken broth into the pot and bring to a simmer.

4. Add in the bay leaves and rice, then mix to combine. Tap Cancel when done.

5. Select the White Rice function, set to Med/Short, then tap Start.

6. Open the lid when 8 minutes remain on the timer and mix in the frozen peas, then add the shrimp on top and close the lid to continue cooking.

SANDWICHES & BURGERS RECIPES

Chick-fil-a Crispy Chicken Sandwich Copycat

Servings: 4

Cooking Time: 10 Minutes

Ingredients:

- 4 chicken breast halves
- 1/2 cup pickle juice
- 1/4 cup water
- 1/2 cup milk
- 1 large egg
- oil for frying
- 4 hamburger buns
- Pickle, lettuce, tomato and cheese slices , for topping
- For the breading:
- 1 cup all-purpose flour
- 3 Tablespoons powdered sugar
- 1/2 teaspoon paprika
- 1 teaspoon freshly ground black pepper
- 1/2 teaspoon chili powder
- 1/2 teaspoon salt
- 1/2 teaspoon baking powder
- 1-2 teaspoons cayenne pepper *optional, for a spicy chicken sandwich
- For the Chick-fil-A-sauce
- 1/2 cup mayonnaise
- 1 teaspoon dijon mustard
- 3 teaspoons yellow mustard
- 2 teaspoon barbecue sauce (hickory tastes the best)
- 2 Tablespoons honey
- 1/2 teaspoon garlic powder
- 1/2 teaspoon paprika
- 1 teaspoon lemon juice

Directions:

1. Marinate the chicken: combine the pickle juice and water in a ziplock bag. Add the chicken breast halves and marinate for 30 minutes.
2. Make the sauce: Make the Chick-fil-A sauce by combining all ingredients in a bowl. Mix well and set aside.
3. Next, in a large bowl mix the breading ingredients together: flour, powdered sugar, paprika, black pepper, chili powder, salt, and baking powder.
4. In another bowl mix the milk, and egg.
5. Add 2-3 cups of oil to a large saucepan and heat oil to about 350 degrees F.
6. Coat the chicken: Dip the marinated chicken into the egg mixture, and then coat in the flour breading mixture. Now "double-dip" by repeating this step and dipping that same chicken tender back into the egg mixture and then back into the flour again!
7. Pan fry: Place chicken in hot oil and fry for 3-4 minutes on each side. Remove to paper towel to dry.
8. Assemble Sandwich: Toast the sandwich buns. Grab the Chick-fil-A sauce and smooth it on both sides of the buns. Top with lettuce, cheese, and crispy chicken! Enjoy!

NOTES

Air Fryer Chick-Fil-A Sandwich:

Preheat fryer to 370°F. Grease the inside basket/rack of the air fryer and place two coated chicken breasts in the air fryer. Lightly spray the top of the chicken. Cook the chicken for 11-13 minutes, flipping halfway through cook time. Assemble sandwich as instructed below.

Baked Chick-Fil-A Sandwich:

Preheat oven to 450°F. Place a wire cooling rack on top of a baking sheet. Place your coated chicken breasts on the wire rack and spray both sides lightly with olive oil. Bake the chicken for 12 minutes, flip and bake for another 15 minutes or until it's cooked through.

For a Spicy Chick-Fil-A Chicken Sandwich:

We love spicy chicken at our house! If you'd like to add a little heat to your chicken sandwich, add 1-2 teaspoons of cayenne pepper to the flour mixture when making the breading. I like to coat my kids sandwiches in the flour first, then add the cayenne for spice, and make mine and my husbands.

Air Fried Peanut Butter And Jelly Sandwich

Servings: 2
Cooking Time: 4 Minutes

Ingredients:

- 2 Tablespoons butter melted
- 4 Tablespoons peanut butter
- 4 Tablespoons grape jelly
- 4 slices bread

Directions:

1. Prepare the air fryer basket with a nonstick cooking spray such as avocado oil or olive oil.
2. Take each slice of bread and butter one side of the bread.
3. Add peanut butter to one piece of bread and jelly to the other piece of bread.
4. Add the peanut butter and jelly together, and place them in a single layer in your prepared air fryer basket.
5. Use the air fry function and fry the sandwiches at 400 degrees Fahrenheit for 3-4 minutes, flipping the sandwich halfway through the cooking time.
6. Remove the sandwich from the air fryer and serve immediately.

NOTES

This recipe was made with a basket style 5.8 qt Cosori air fryer. If you are using a different brand of air fryer, you may need to adjust the cooking time accordingly. All air fryers cook a little differently, and it's always best to check a recipe by making a test run so you can adjust the cooking time as needed.

Use your favorite jam or favorite jelly that you and your family love, but also consider going outside of the box with this pb&j sandwich.

I love to use the class white bread, but you can also use wheat bread or sourdough bread or any of your favorite pieces of bread with this recipe.

Sunny Side Burgers

Servings: 4

Ingredients:

- Oil spray
- 2 teaspoons kosher salt
- 1 teaspoon ground black pepper
- ½ teaspoon onion powder
- ½ teaspoon garlic powder
- 1 pound ground angus beef
- 4 sunny side up fried eggs, with runny yolks
- 4 slices Munster cheese, or cheese of choice
- 2 cups caramelized onion
- 2 tablespoons mayonnaise
- 4 Brioche burger buns, sliced
- Boston bib lettuce, as needed
- Tomato slices, as needed
- 2 teaspoons crushed red pepper flakes, for garnish
- Ketchup, for serving
- Yellow mustard, for serving

Directions:

1. Combine the kosher salt, ground black pepper, onion powder, and garlic powder together in a large bowl. Mix the spices into the ground angus beef and then form into four quarter pound patties, about a ½-inch thick.
2. Place the cooking pot into the base of the Indoor Grill, followed by the grill plate.
3. Select the Air Grill function on max heat, adjust the temperature to 510F and cooking time to 7 minutes, press Shake, then press Start/Pause.
4. Note: This will yieldamedium-rare burger.Spray the grill grate lightly with oil spray once the grill is done preheating.
5. Place the burger patties onto the preheated grill grate and press Start/Pause. Flip the patties when the Shake reminder beeps.

6. Add the cheese to the patties when 2 minutes remain on the timer.

7. Remove when done and set onto a wire rack to rest.

8. Spread the mayonnaise over the insides of the sliced Brioche buns.

9. Select the Broil function, adjust time to 3 minutes, press the Preheat button to cancel the automatic preheat, then place the buns mayonnaise side down onto the grill plate. Press Start/Pause then close the lid to begin cooking.

10. Remove the buns when toasted and set aside until cool to the touch.

11. Assemble the burgers by topping the bottom halves of the brioche buns with lettuce and tomato, then place the burger patty on top followed by caramelized onions, then the sunny side up fried egg, sprinkle with crushed red pepper flakes, and finish with the top half of the bun.

12. Serve immediately with the condiments on the side and pair with hashbrowns or home fries, and fresh fruit.

Air Fryer Hamburgers

Servings: 4
Cooking Time: 12 Minutes

Ingredients:

- 4 hamburger patties

Directions:

1. Preheat the Air Fryer to 370 degrees Fahrenheit. Prepare the Air Fryer basket with nonstick cooking spray.

2. Add the hamburger patties into the Air Fryer basket in a single layer.

3. Cook in the preheated fryer for 6 minutes. Flip the hamburger patties and cook for an additional 5-7 minutes, dependending on how well done you would like the hamburgers.

4. Carefully remove the hamburger patties from the Air Fryer basket and serve with your favorite sides and toppings.

NOTES

If cooking frozen hamburger patties, add an extra minute or two to the cook time to ensure they are cooked thoroughly.

Air Fryer Salmon Fish Sandwich

Servings: 4
Cooking Time: 10 Minutes

Ingredients:

- Lemon-Caper Mayo:
- 6 tbsp mayonnaise (I like Sir Kensington)
- 2 tablespoons drained capers (minced)
- 2 teaspoons fresh lemon juice
- For the Fish:
- 16 ounces skinless salmon fillet (if frozen thawed, cut in 4 pieces)
- 1 teaspoon kosher salt (divided)
- 2 large egg whites (lightly beaten)
- 1 cup seasoned panko* (or gluten free panko)
- Olive oil spray
- 4 whole wheat buns (or gluten free buns)
- 4 butter lettuce leaves

Directions:

1. Combine the ingredients for the Lemon-Caper Mayo in a small bowl and refrigerate until ready to eat.

2. Pat the salmon dry with a paper towel. Cut the fish into 4 pieces, about 4 x 4 inches. Season with 1/2 teaspoon salt.

3. Place the egg whites in a shallow bowl.

4. In a second shallow bowl combine the panko with remaining 1/2 teaspoon salt.

5. Dip the fish into the egg whites, then the panko. Set aside.

6. Spray the basket with oil. Lay the fish on the basket in a single layer, in batches as needed.

7. Spray the tops of the fish with oil and air fry 400F 8 minutes, turning half way, until golden and crisp.

8. Serve fish on buns with lettuce and divide the sauce.

Best Ever Grilled Cheese Sandwiches

Servings: 2

Ingredients:

- 2 tablespoons mayonnaise
- 1 teaspoon Dijon mustard
- 4 slices sourdough bread
- 2 slices Swiss cheese
- 2 slices cheddar cheese
- 2 slices sweet onion
- 1 medium tomato, sliced
- 6 cooked bacon strips
- 2 tablespoons butter, softened

Directions:

1. Combine mayonnaise and mustard; spread over 2 bread slices. Layer with cheeses, onion, tomato and bacon; top with remaining bread. Spread outsides of sandwiches with butter.
2. In a small skillet over medium heat, toast sandwiches until cheese is melted, 2-3 minutes on each side.

Air Fryer Cheeseburgers

Servings: 4
Cooking Time: 30 Minutes

Ingredients:

- 500 grams minced beef
- 1 egg
- ¾ cup (75g) panko breadcrumbs
- 2 tablespoons barbecue sauce
- 1 tablespoon smoked paprika
- 1 clove garlic, crushed
- ¼ cup (70g) low-sugar tomato sauce
- 4 large brioche buns (400g)
- olive oil cooking spray
- 4 slices cheddar
- 4 centre-cut bacon rashers (140g)
- 2 tablespoons whole-egg mayonnaise
- 4 baby cos lettuce leaves
- 1/3 cup (40g) burger pickles
- to serve: sweet potato chips

Directions:

1. Using your hands, combine beef, egg, breadcrumbs, barbecue sauce, paprika, garlic and 1 tablespoon of the tomato sauce in a large bowl, then season; mix well. Shape mixture into four patties the same size as the brioche buns; ensure they will all fit into the air fryer basket. Spray all over with cooking spray.
2. Preheat a 7-litre air fryer to 180°C/350°F for 3 minutes.
3. Spray the air fryer basket with cooking spray. Taking care, place patties in the basket; at 180°C/350°F, cook for 10 minutes, turning halfway through cooking time, or until browned and cooked through. Transfer to a plate and top each with a slice of cheddar; cover loosely with foil to keep warm.
4. Arrange bacon in the air fryer basket. Reset the temperature to 200°C/400°F; cook for 5 minutes until crisp.
5. Split and toast brioche buns. Spread bun bases with mayonnaise, then top with lettuce, patties, bacon, pickles and remaining tomato sauce; sandwich together with bun tops.
6. Serve cheeseburgers with sweet potato chips.

Air Fryer Burgers

Servings: 4
Cooking Time: 12 Minutes

Ingredients:

- 1 lb ground hamburger recommend 85/15
- 1 tsp Worcestershire sauce
- 1 tsp seasoning salt
- 1 tsp garlic powder
- 1 tsp onion powder
- 4 slices cheese
- 4 buns
- *additional toppings like lettuce tomatoes, pickles, bacon ketchup, mustard. mayonnaise etc.

Directions:

1. In a large mixing bowl combine hamburger, Worcestershire sauce, seasoning salt, garlic powder and onion powder and combine with hands. Do not overmix. Form into 4 patties.
2. Place the burgers in the air fryer, you may have to cook two at a time depending on the size of your air fryer.
3. Cook the burgers for 8 minutes at 360 degrees F. Flip the burgers over and cook for an additional 6-8 minutes or until the internal temperature of the burgers are 160 degrees F.
4. Top each burger with a slice of cheese and cook for an additional minute or until the cheese is melted.
5. Serve on buns with your favorite condiments.

NOTES

Press a thumbprint into the middle of each patty before it goes in the air fryer. This will help the patty hold it's shape rather than shrinking as it cooks.

Air Fryer Frozen Burgers

Servings: 4
Cooking Time: 15 Minutes

Ingredients:

- 4 beef burger patties

Directions:

1. There is no need to preheat the air fryer for this and no oil needed too, simply place the frozen burger patties in the air fryer.
2. Cook the burgers for 15 minutes at 180C/360F flipping once for even cooking. If you would be topping the burger with cheese, add it 30 seconds or 1 minute before the end of the cooking time and cook until the cheese melts. I mostly do 30 seconds.
3. If cooking thinner patties then cook for 10 minutes at180C/360F. The internal temperature of well done burger should register 160F/71C
4. Carefully remove the cooked burger from the air fryer basket and assemble on hamburger buns with other toppings of choice. Enjoy!
5. PS: the burger shrinks when cooked so don't be alarmed if this happens

NOTES

Estimated nutritional value provided for hamburger patties only.

BEEF, PORK & LAMB RECIPES

Air Fryer Bacon-wrapped Figs

Servings: 12
Cooking Time: 10 Minutes

Ingredients:

- 12 dried Turkish or mission figs
- 6 strips regular center-cut bacon (not thick cut)
- Goat cheese or blue cheese for stuffing, optional
- Salted, roasted almonds for stuffing, optional
- Honey, for serving
- Nonstick spray, for air fryer

Directions:

1. Reconstitute the figs:
2. Add the dried figs to a bowl filled with steaming hot water. Let them sit for 20 minutes to reconstitute. Drain the figs and cut off the stems. Cut a small slit in each fig and spoon in a little blue cheese or goat cheese, or half an almond, if desired. You could also do a mix of fillings.
3. Wrap the bacon around the figs:
4. Cut the strips of bacon in half and trim them down to about 1/2 to 3/4 inches wide. Wrap one bacon strip around each fig. Secure with a toothpick.
5. Air fry the figs:
6. Spray the basket of your air fryer with nonstick spray. Add bacon-wrapped figs in a single layer so they aren't touching. Air fry the figs at 350 ℉ for 8-9 minutes, flipping once halfway through.
7. If you don't have an air fryer, broil the figs on high for about 3 minutes per side.
8. Serve the figs:
9. Once the figs have cooled slightly, serve them drizzled with honey.
10. Leftover figs (yeah right!) will keep in the fridge for up to 5 days. Reheat in a 350 ℉ oven, or reheat in the air fryer for a few minutes before eating.

Air Fryer London Broil

Servings: 4
Cooking Time: 10 Minutes

Ingredients:

- 1 1/2 pound London broil
- 2 Tablespoons olive oil extra virgin
- 1/2 teaspoon ground black pepper
- 1 teaspoon garlic powder
- 1 teaspoon onion powder
- 1/2 teaspoon parsley fresh, chopped

Directions:

1. Preheat your air fryer to 400° F/200 C for 5 minutes.
2. In a small bowl, combine the ground black pepper, garlic powder, and onion powder together. Set bowl aside.
3. On a cutting board pat the steak dry with paper towels.
4. Then use a sharp knife and trim any excess pieces off of the steak.
5. Rub all sides of the steak with light olive oil. Then rub the seasoning mixture all over the steak.
6. Place seasoned steak into the preheated air fryer basket.
7. Cooking time is 8-10 minutes at 400°F/200 C. Depending on your level of doneness to get the perfect temperature.
8. Then flip the steak and cook for an additional 2 minutes.
9. To get the perfect cook on your steak use an internal read thermometer to get your desired degree of doneness.
10. Let the steak rest for 10 minutes on a cooling rack.
11. Lastly cut the steak into thin slices and garnish with chopped parsley, a pat of butter, and then serve.

NOTES

I make this recipe in my basket style 5.8 qt Cosori air fryer. Depending on your air fryer, size and wattage the cook time will vary 2-3 minutes.

Temperature guidelines are as follows for a great cooked steak so use an instant-read meat thermometer or digital thermometer when air frying. For best results, to cook your perfect steak the internal temperature should read 120-125 degrees F for rare, medium rare 130-135 degrees F, medium doneness will read 140-145 degrees F, medium well 150-155 degrees F and well done will be 160 degrees F.

Consider an optional dipping sauce such as a decadent cowboy butter sauce, ranch dressing, a velvety cheese sauce, garlic, a few tablespoons of lemon juice, a sour cream mixture, or a blue cheese dressing.

Carnitas

Servings: 4-6
Cooking Time: 45 Minutes

Ingredients:

- 3 pounds (1½ kilograms) pork butt or shoulder
- 2 tablespoons (30 grams) orange zest
- 7 garlic cloves, crushed
- 1 large yellow onion, small diced
- 1 serrano pepper, deveined and deseeded, cut into ¼-inch (6-millimeter) strips
- 1½ teaspoons (8 grams) dried oregano leaves
- 1 teaspoon (5 grams) ground cumin
- 2 bay leaves
- 2 teaspoons (10 grams) kosher salt, plus more to taste
- 2 teaspoons (10 grams) ground black pepper
- 1½ cup (354 milliliters) water
- ½ cup (118 milliliters) fresh orange juice
- 1 cinnamon stick
- 12 small corn tortillas, warmed, for serving
- Cilantro, chopped, for garnish
- Onion, chopped, for garnish
- Salsa roja, for serving
- Salsa verde, for serving

Directions:

1. Trim any excess fat from the pork and slice into 4 equal portions. Discard any pieces of pure fat.
2. Combine the pork with the orange zest, garlic, onion, serrano pepper, oregano, cumin, bay leaves, salt, and black pepper.
3. Place the pork into the Smart Air Fryer basket, without the crisper plate.
4. Pour the water and orange juice over the top of the pork, add the cinnamon stick, then insert the basket into the air fryer.
5. Select the Roast function, adjust temperature to 375°F and time to 45 minutes, then press Start/Pause.
6. Flip the pork pieces halfway through cooking and stir the contents of the basket until evenly mixed.
7. Remove the pork when done and allow to rest for 10 minutes before shredding.
8. Serve immediately with tortillas, cilantro, onion, salsa roja, and salsa verde if desired as the main ingredient for a taco, burrito, rice bowl, or topping for a salad.

Lamb Cutlets With Crumbed Eggplant And Pesto

Servings: 4
Cooking Time: 15 Minutes

Ingredients:

- Lamb cutlets with crumbed eggplant and pesto
- 1/4 cup (60g) olive oil
- 12 french-trimmed lamb cutlets (600g)
- 1 egg
- 2 tablespoon milk
- 2 tablespoon plain (all-purpose) flour
- 1 1/2 cup (100g) panko (japanese) breadcrumbs
- 1 medium eggplant (300g)
- 1 tablespoon olive oil, extra
- 1/3 cup (90g) pesto
- 250 gram rocket leaves (arugula)

Directions:

1. Lamb cutlets with crumbed eggplant and pesto
2. Heat 1 tablespoon of the oil in a large frying pan over high heat. Season lamb, cook lamb, for 3 minutes each side or until browned and cooked as desired. Remove from pan, cover to keep warm.
3. Meanwhile, lightly beat egg and milk in a shallow bowl. Place flour and breadcrumbs in separate shallow bowls.
4. Thickly slice eggplant, pat dry with paper towel. Dip eggplant in flour, shake off excess, dip in egg mixture, then coat in breadcrumbs.
5. Heat remaining oil in same pan, over medium heat, cook eggplant, in batches, for 2 minutes each side or until browned lightly. Drain on paper towel.
6. Drizzle extra oil over pesto. Serve lamb with eggplant and rocket, accompany with pesto.

NOTES

Store bought pesto is available from the refrigerated section of most supermarkets (near the dips). You will also find it in the pasta aisle.

Air Fryer Bacon Wrapped Tater Tots

Servings: 4
Cooking Time: 14 Minutes

Ingredients:

* 24 frozen tater tots
* 12 slices bacon
* 1/4 cup brown sugar

Directions:

1. Cut each slice of bacon in half, making 24 bacon slices.
2. Wrap one piece of bacon strip around one tater tot. Seal ends together with toothpicks if necessary.
3. In a medium bowl, toss bacon wrapped tots with brown sugar to coat.
4. Place coated tots in the air fryer basket, without stacking or overlapping.

5. Air fry at 350 degrees F for 14-16 minutes, until bacon reaches your desired crispness, and tater tots are cooked through.

NOTES

Optional Favorite Dipping Sauce: Hot onion dip, ranch dressing, honey mustard, blue cheese dressing or sriracha aioli.

Optional Additional Toppings: Honey glaze, green onions or chives, spicy maple glaze, shredded cheese or grated parmesan cheese.

Cooking Tips: Use a silicone baking mat for easy clean up.

Bacon Wrapped Green Bean Bundles

Servings: 12
Cooking Time: 30 Minutes

Ingredients:

* 6 slices bacon
* 1 ½ pounds green beans 6-8 beans per bundle
* ½ teaspoon baking soda
* ¼ teaspoon garlic powder
* salt & pepper to taste
* 1 tablespoon brown sugar

Directions:

1. Preheat oven to 375°F.
2. Cook bacon on the stovetop until slightly cooked (not crispy), about 3-4 minutes. Reserve any drippings.
3. Trim and wash green beans. Bring a large pot of water to a boil, add baking soda. Add green beans and cook 3 minutes until tender-crisp. Remove from boiling water and place in a bowl of ice water to stop cooking.
4. Dab beans dry and toss with reserved bacon drippings (about 2 teaspoons) or olive oil if you don't have drippings, garlic powder, and salt & pepper to taste.

5. Cut each slice of bacon in half and wrap around about 6-8 green beans, secure with a toothpick, and place on a parchment-lined pan.

6. Combine brown sugar with 1 tablespoon of water and lightly brush over each bundle.

7. Roast 20-22 minutes or until bacon is crisp and beans are lightly roasted.

NOTES

Pre-cook the bacon so that a lot of the fat is removed. This will help it crisp without overcooking the beans.

These can be oven roasted or cooked in the air fryer at 380°F for about 11-13 minutes.

Pre-cooked bacon can be used in place of raw bacon.

Blanch (boil and then ice bath) the green beans for the best texture. Be sure to dry them well before wrapping.

Prep ahead and bake at the last minute.

Reheat in the oven at 375°F on a parchment-lined pan until heated through.

Air-fryer Spicy Ginger Beef Skewers

Servings: 6
Cooking Time: 5 Minutes

Ingredients:

- 1 beef flank steak (1-1/2 pounds)
- 1 cup rice vinegar
- 1 cup soy sauce
- 1/4 cup packed brown sugar
- 2 tablespoons minced fresh gingerroot
- 6 garlic cloves, minced
- 3 teaspoons sesame oil
- 2 teaspoons Sriracha chili sauce or 1 teaspoon hot pepper sauce
- 1/2 teaspoon cornstarch
- Optional: Sesame seeds and thinly sliced green onions

Directions:

1. Cut beef into 1/4-in.-thick strips. In a large bowl, whisk the next 7 ingredients until blended. Pour 1 cup marinade into a shallow dish. Add beef; turn to coat. Cover and refrigerate 2-8 hours. Cover and refrigerate remaining marinade.

2. Preheat air fryer to 400◆◆. Drain beef, discarding marinade in dish. Thread beef onto 12 metal or soaked wooden skewers that fit into air fryer. Working in batches if necessary, arrange skewers in a single layer on greased tray in air-fryer basket. Cook until meat reaches desired doneness (for medium-rare, a thermometer should read 135◆◆; medium, 140◆◆; medium-well, 145◆◆), 4-5 minutes, turning occasionally and basting frequently, using 1/2 cup of reserved marinade.

3. Meanwhile, to make glaze, bring remaining marinade (about 3/4 cup) to a boil; whisk in 1/2 teaspoon cornstarch. Cook, whisking constantly, until thickened, 1-2 minutes. Brush skewers with glaze just before serving. If desired, top with sesame seeds and sliced green onions.

Air-fried Mini Italian Meatloaves Stuffed With Cheese

Servings: 4

Ingredients:

- 1 egg, lightly beaten
- ⅓ cup milk
- 1 clove garlic, minced
- 2 tablespoon purchased basil pesto
- ¼ teaspoon black pepper
- 1 pound 90% lean ground beef
- ⅓ cup Italian seasoned fine dry bread crumbs
- 8 slices pepperoni
- 2 ounce fresh mozzarella pearls (such as BelGioioso)
- ½ cup marinara sauce, warmed
- Chopped fresh basil (optional)
- Grated Parmesan (optional)

Directions:

1. In a medium bowl combine first 5 ingredients (through pepper). Add ground beef and bread crumbs. Combine, being careful not to overmix.

2. Divide meat mixture into four portions. Press a well into each portion, leaving 1/2-inch border around the edge. Place 2 slices of pepperoni in each well, shingling to cover the length of the well. Top each with about 6 mozzarella pearls. Press meat mixture around the filling to enclose. Shape each portion into an oblong loaf shape.

3. Place loaves in basket of air fryer, in batches. Cook at 370°F for about 15 minutes or until an instant-read thermometer inserted in the thickest portion of meat reaches 165°F. Serve topped with warm marinara sauce, fresh basil and Parmesan, if desired.

Air Fryer Stuffed Peppers

Servings: 4
Cooking Time: 12 Minutes

Ingredients:

- 4 bell peppers
- 1 pound of lean ground beef
- 1 cup of cooked rice
- 1 Tablespoon of olive oil
- 2 cups of tomato sauce
- ½ onion, chopped
- ½ Tablespoon minced garlic
- Salt and pepper to taste
- 1 teaspoon of Italian seasoning
- ¾ cup of shredded mozzarella
- Optional: parsley for garnish

Directions:

1. Preheat your air fryer to 300 degrees.

2. Cut the tops of the peppers off and then scrape out the seeds.

3. Cook your rice according to the package directions.

4. Brush your peppers with olive oil, inside and out. Place them into the air fryer basket and cook for 5 minutes.

5. While the peppers are cooking, season your beef with salt and pepper then brown it with the onions and garlic, in a medium saucepan, over medium high heat. Cook till there is no more pink in the beef and then drain the grease.

6. Add the cooked rice, tomato sauce, and Italian seasoning to your beef mixture and simmer for 4 minutes.

7. Scoop the beef mixture into the peppers and place them back into the air fryer. Cook at 350 degrees for 8 minutes. Top them with the shredded mozzarella and place back into the air fryer for another 3-4 minutes, till the tops are golden brown.

8. Remove from the air fryer and enjoy. Top with chopped parsley for additional garnish.

Air Fryer Steak Kabobs

Servings: 4
Cooking Time: 10 Minutes

Ingredients:

- 15 oz steak
- 1 red bell pepper
- 1 green bell pepper
- 1 red onion
- olive oil
- 2 Tbsp soy sauce

Directions:

1. Preheat the Air Fryer to 400 degrees Fahrenheit. Prepare the Air Fryer basket with a non stick spray such as olive oil or avocado oil.

2. Cube the steak into bite-sized pieces and soak them in the soy sauce while cutting up the vegetables.

3. Cut the bell peppers and onion into bite-sized pieces.

4. Grab a skewer and rotate adding the steak, onion, and peppers, and then repeat until you've reached the end of the skewer.

5. Place the steak skewers in a single layer in the prepared Air Fryer basket. Cook on 400 degrees

Fahrenheit for 10 minutes, flipping the skewers after 5 minutes.

6. Serve alone, with dipping sauce, or with your favorite sides.

NOTES

You can store leftovers in an airtight container in the refrigerator for up to 3 days. To reheat, place them in a preheated air fryer at 400 degrees Fahrenheit for 3-4 minutes, or until heated fully through.

The best meat choice is the cuts of steak you prefer the most! I personally prefer top sirloin, ribeye, and New York strip steaks for the best beef kebabs. You can also a cheaper cut of meat such as stew meat.

Choice easy seasonings such as soy sauce, Worcestershire sauce, and teriyaki sauce. You can also choose to use garlic powder, steak seasoning,

Would you rather chicken? You can use chicken rather than steak. Cube the chicken breasts into bite sized pieces and add them to the skewer in place of the steak, or even in addition to the steak

Steak Tacos With A Pineapple Salsa

Ingredients:

- Marinade
- 1 lb. skirt steak
- 1/4 cup jalapeno, diced
- 2 cloves garlic, minced
- 1/4 cup cilantro, chopped
- 3 Tbsp lime juice
- 3 Tbsp olive oil
- 1 tsp salt
- 1/2 tsp pepper
- 1/2 tsp cumin
- Pineapple Salsa
- 1 cup pineapple, diced
- 1 Tbsp jalapeno, diced
- 1/4 cup red onion, diced
- 1/4 cup cilantro, chopped
- 1 garlic clove, minced

- 1 Tbsp lime juice
- Salt, to taste

Directions:

1. Combine all of the marinade ingredients together into a Ziploc bag. Add in the skirt steak and shake to coat in the marinade.

2. Marinate for at least one hour in the fridge. Remove it from the fridge and let it come to temperature before cooking.

3. Preheat the Air Fryer to 400F.

4. Add the steak to the basket and cook for about 11 minutes, flipping halfway. This is dependent on the size of your steak and how you enjoy it cooked. We had ours medium rare.

5. Dice all the ingredients for the Pineapple Salsa topping and combine everything in a bowl and mix. Set aside.

6. Remove the steak and let it rest for about 5-7 minutes and then slice.

7. Assemble the tacos and enjoy!

Reheat Ribs In The Air Fryer

Servings: 2-3
Cooking Time: 5 Minutes

Ingredients:

- 1 pound leftover ribs (can use more or less)

Directions:

1. Preheat your air fryer to 380 degrees F.

2. Lay the ribs in a single layer in the air fryer basket.*

3. Cook for about 5-7 minutes, until warmed thoroughly.

NOTES

* if reheating sauced ribs in the air fryer, I recommend using an air fryer pan, or parchment round/silicone liner to help with clean up.

HOW TO REHEAT PRIME RIB IN THE AIR FRYER:

Preheat the air fryer to 270 degrees F.

Lay the prime rib in a single layer (use a parchment round or silicone liner if it's sauced).

Cook for about 10 minutes.

Breaded Pork Cutlets With Lime

Servings: 4
Cooking Time: 15 Minutes

Ingredients:

- 4 5 oz thin sliced lean pork sirloin cutlets
- seasoned salt (such as adobo)
- 2 large egg whites (beaten)
- 1/2 teaspoon sazon (homemade or packaged)
- 1/2 cup seasoned breadcrumbs (or gluten-free crumbs)
- 1 1/2 tbsp olive oil
- lime wedges for serving

Directions:

1. Season cutlets with 3/4 teaspoon seasoned salt.
2. Place bread crumbs in a medium shallow bowl.
3. In another bowl beat egg whites with sazon.
4. Dip pork cutlets in egg whites, then breadcrumb mixture, shaking off excess.
5. Heat a large nonstick frying pan on medium to medium heat. Add the olive oil and pork cutlets, cook about 6 minutes on each side, until golden brown and no longer pink in the center.
6. Serve with lime wedges.
7. Air Fryer Directions:
8. After cutlets are breaded spray both sides with oil and air fry at 400F for 4 minutes on each side, or until golden

Beef & Broccoli

Servings: 4

Ingredients:

- 1 tbsp garlic powder
- 90ml sweet soy sauce
- 1 tsp crushed chillies (optional)
- 500g uncooked sirloin steak, thinly sliced
- 300ml teriyaki sauce or marinade, divided
- 1 head of broccoli (250g), cut in 2cm florets
- 1 tbsp vegetable oil
- 1 tsp sea salt
- 1 tsp ground black pepper
- 2 tbsp water
- Cooked rice, for serving

Directions:

1. In a large mixing bowl, mix together garlic powder, sweet soy sauce, crushed chillies, steak and half of the marinade. Let marinate in the fridge for at least 30 minutes or up to 24 hours. After marinating, strain beef and discard excess marinade.
2. In a large mixing bowl, toss the broccoli with the vegetable oil, salt and pepper.
3. Remove the crisper plate from the basket. Preheat the unit by selecting ROAST, setting the temperature to 190°C and setting the time to 5 minutes. Select START/STOP to begin.
4. After 5 minutes, add the water and broccoli to the pan; reinsert pan. Select ROAST, set temperature to 190°C, and set time to 11 minutes. Select START/STOP to begin.
5. After 6 minutes, remove the pan. Add beef on top of the broccoli and resume cooking.
6. Cook the beef and broccoli for another 5 minutes, rotating once after 2 minutes and another time after 4 minutes.
7. When cooking is complete, serve immediately with additional teriyaki sauce and steamed rice.

Air Fryer Frozen Steak

Servings: 2
Cooking Time: 10 Minutes

Ingredients:

- 1 pound ribeye steak (bone-in or boneless), 1-inch thick
- ½ tablespoon olive oil (or spray)
- 1 teaspoon garlic powder, or to taste
- ½ teaspoon dried rosemary, or to taste
- ½ teaspoon kosher salt, or to taste
- ½ teaspoon black pepper, or to taste

- Butter, for serving

Directions:

1. Brush (or spray) the frozen steak with olive oil on both sides, then sprinkle the steak with salt, pepper, rosemary, and garlic powder.
2. place the steak inside. Air fry at 400 degrees F for 18-30 minutes (depending on thickness), flipping once halfway until it is done to your liking.*
3. Allow the steak to rest in the warm air fryer for 3-5 minutes, then use a thermometer to check the internal temperature to check that it is at your desired temp, then serve it with a pat of butter.

NOTES

*Rare (125-130F) - 8-10 minutes per side

Medium (140-150F) - 11-12 minutes per side

Well (160F+) - 12-15 minutes per side

HOW TO REHEAT STEAK IN THE AIR FRYER:

Preheat your air fryer to 350 degrees.

Cook steak in the air fryer for 3 to 5 minutes until heated thoroughly, let sit fot 5 minutes, then enjoy!

Bacon Cheddar Cauliflower Tots

Servings: 4

Cooking Time: 45 Minutes

Ingredients:

- 2 pounds cauliflower florets
- 1 ½ teaspoons kosher salt divided
- 8 ounces sharp cheddar cheese shredded (approx 2 cups)
- 12 bacon strips cooked and crumbled
- ¼ cup cornmeal
- 2 eggs
- 1 teaspoon mustard powder
- ½ teaspoon garlic powder
- ½ teaspoon onion powder
- ½ teaspoon cayenne pepper

Directions:

1. Using a grater, grate the florets until they are the size of cooked rice grains. Put the cauliflower into a bowl that is lined with a clean kitchen towel.
2. Sprinkle 1 teaspoon of salt over the cauliflower and let it sit at room temperature for 5 minutes. Fold the towel ends over the top of the bowl and microwave it for 2 minutes.
3. Remove from the microwave and unfold the towel letting it cool down until it is comfortable to handle. Once cool, gather up the towel ends and twist while squeezing the cooked cauliflower to remove as much moisture as possible.
4. Preheat the oven to 425°F. Line two half-sheet pans with parchment paper.
5. Empty any liquid that remains in the bowl and add the cooked cauliflower into it, add the remaining ingredients and stir vigorously until fully combined.
6. Use a small cookie scoop to portion the mixture and place 1 ½ inches apart on the prepared pan to allow room for spreading. Gently pat the tots to flatten slightly.
7. Bake for 25 minutes or until golden brown on top with a dark brown on the bottom.
8. Let the tots stand for 2 minutes on the pan before serving.

NOTES

These can be cooked in an air fryer at 400°F for 12 minutes (flip after 6 minutes).

Be sure to squeeze the cauliflower very dry.

Easy Pork Dumplings

Servings: 48

Ingredients:

- DUMPLINGS
- 4 hot or sweet Italian sausages, casings removed
- 4 scallions, finely chopped
- 3 tablespoons chopped fresh cilantro
- 1 large egg, beaten
- 1 tablespoon soy sauce
- 1 tablespoon grated fresh ginger (from a 2-in. piece)

- 1 teaspoon toasted sesame oil
- 48 round wonton wrappers (from a 14-oz. pkg.)
- Vegetable oil, for cooking
- DIPPING SAUCE
- 2 tablespoons soy sauce
- 1 tablespoon rice vinegar
- 1 scallion, thinly sliced
- 1 teaspoon granulated sugar
- 1 teaspoon toasted sesame oil

Directions:

1. Make The Dumplings Line A Large Baking Sheet With Parchment Paper. Using A Fork, Stir Together Sausage, Scallions, Cilantro, Egg, Soy Sauce, Ginger, And Sesame Oil In A Large Bowl. Fill A Small Bowl With Water. Lay 3 Wonton Wrappers On A Work Surface. Place 1 Rounded Teaspoon Of Sausage Mixture In The Center Of Each Wrapper. Dip A Finger In Water And Rub Around The Edge Of Each Wrapper. Fold 1 Side Of Wrapper Over Filling. Make 3 Pleats Along Seam And Pinch To Seal. Transfer Assembled Dumplings To Prepared Baking Sheet. Repeat With Remaining Sausage Mixture And Wrappers.Add Water To A Medium Nonstick Skillet Until Bottom Is Just Covered; Bring To A Simmer Over Medium-High. Add As Many Dumplings, Flat Side Down, As Will Comfortably Fit. Cover And Steam Until Wrappers Are Translucent, About 3 Minutes.Pour Off Any Water Remaining In Skillet. Add 2 Tablespoons Vegetable Oil (If Dumplings Are Sticking, Shake Skillet Gently Or Loosen Dumplings With A Rubber Spatula). Cook, Undisturbed, Until Bottoms Are Golden And Crispy, About 1 Minute. Transfer Dumplings To A Paper Towel– Lined Plate. Wipe Skillet Clean And Repeat With Water, Remaining Dumplings, And Vegetable Oil.
2. Make The Dipping Sauces Tir Together All Ingredients Plus 1 Tablespoon Water In A Small Bowl Until Sugar Dissolves. Serve With Dumplings
3. To Freezet Ransfer Uncooked Dumplings On Baking Sheet To Freezer. Freeze, Uncovered, Until Firm, About 2 Hours. Remove Frozen Dumplings From Baking Sheet And Transfer To A Resealable Plastic Bag. Freeze For Up To 3 Months. Cook As Directed (Do Not Thaw), Adding 2 To 3 Minutes To Steam Time.

Air Fryer Meatballs & Pasta Machine Spaghetti

Servings: 4
Cooking Time: 5 Minutes

Ingredients:

- 1 cup flour
- ½ cup water

Directions:

1. Use the cups that come with the machine.
2. Fill the flour one to the top - don't pack.
3. Fill the water container to the first line
4. Put the flour in the machine and select 1 cup and start
5. Pour the water in after it starts on the side
6. Run the machine
7. After three minutes start cutting the pasta.

Air Fryer T-bone Steak

Servings: 4

Ingredients:

- 2 T-Bone Steaks
- 1 tablespoon olive oil
- 1/2 teaspoon kosher salt
- 1/2 teaspoon black pepper

Directions:

1. Pat steaks dry with a paper towel and rest T bone steaks on the counter or a cutting board for 15-20 minutes prior to cooking because it allows the steaks to reach room temperature so it will cook more evenly.
2. Lightly brush steaks with olive oil, and then season with salt and pepper on both sides.

3. Place steaks in basket, without stacking or overlapping.

4. Air fry steaks at 400 degrees F, for 6-8 minutes on each side, depending on preference of doneness. Use a reliable meat thermometer to check internal temperature of meat. Garnish steaks with parsley flakes, or with peppercorn sauce.

5. Let steaks rest for 5-10 minutes before serving because this allows excess juices from steak to redistribute and keep meat super moist.

NOTES

Optional Favorite Steak Rubs: I use good old salt & pepper to season steaks. But Italian seasoning, a pinch of cayenne pepper or red pepper flakes, herbs de Provence or dry mustard, can all add a little extra flavor.

Optional Favorite Steak Seasonings and Toppings: Steak sauce, garlic butter, fresh herbs with sautéed mushrooms, crispy herbs, creamy blue cheese, chimichurri or a fresh tomato and basil salad.

Optional Dipping Sauces: Steak sauce, creamed horseradish, teriyaki sauce, burgundy mushroom sauce, miso ginger or pesto sauce.

Kitchen Tips: Thicker steaks will take an additional 3-4 minutes to reach your desired temperature. You can make a garlic herb compound butter days in advance to top steak with. Frozen steaks turn out incredible when cooked in the air fryer.

Air Fryer Ham Steaks

Servings: 2
Cooking Time: 10 Minutes

Ingredients:

- 1 ham steak (about 1/2 inch thick, 1/2 lb. (1.25 cm - 227g))
- 2 Tablespoons (30 ml) melted butter
- 1 Tablespoon (15 ml) brown sugar
- 1 teaspoon (5 ml) honey
- 1 Tablespoon (15 ml) orange juice, pineapple juice or apple juice
- 1 teaspoon (5 ml) mustard (optional)

Directions:

1. Make the glaze: In bowl mix melted butter, brown sugar, honey, juice, and optional mustard.

2. Cut ham into steaks if needed. Make sure they are a size that will fit in your air fryer. Brush both sides of ham steak with glaze.

3. Place ham steak in a single layer in air fryer basket/rack. Air fry at 380°F/193°C for about 5 minutes.

4. Flip the steaks and brush a little more glaze on top. Air fry for another 2-4 minutes or until the ham is brown and cooked to your liking.

5. Brush with remaining glaze if desired before serving the ham.

SALADS & SIDE DISHES RECIPES

Air Fryer Artichokes

Servings: 6
Cooking Time: 16 Minutes

Ingredients:

- 3 medium artichokes
- 1 small lemon, juiced (3 tablespoons lemon juice)
- 1 tablespoon olive oil
- Kosher salt, to taste
- Black pepper, to taste

Directions:

1. Preheat your air fryer to 340 degrees F.
2. Rinse the artichokes, then trim the stems and remove the tough outer leaves. Cut them in half lengthwise and remove the fuzzy choke from the inside using a spoon.
3. Pour the lemon juice over the cut sides. Drizzle with olive oil and season with salt and pepper, to taste. Flip them and repeat on the leafy side.
4. Place them cut side down in the air fryer and fry for 12 minutes. Open the air fryer, flip the artichokes, then fry for 4 more minutes.
5. Serve with lemon wedges and your favorite dipping sauce.

Fried Cauliflower

Servings: 4
Cooking Time: 35 Minutes

Ingredients:

- Fried cauliflower
- 2 eggs
- 1/2 cup (110 grams) self-raising flour
- 1/2 cup (125 millilitres) water
- 1/3 cup finely chopped fresh coriander
- vegetable oil, for deep-frying
- 1 small cauliflower, cut into small florets
- 1 cup (280 grams) greek-style yoghurt

Directions:

1. Fried cauliflower
2. In a medium shallow bowl, whisk eggs, flour and the water until batter is smooth. Stir in half the coriander; season.
3. Heat oil in wok. Dip cauliflower in batter; drain off excess. Deep-fry cauliflower, in batches, until browned lightly and tender. Drain on absorbent paper.
4. In a small bowl, combine remaining coriander and yoghurt; season to taste.
5. Serve cauliflower with coriander yoghurt.

Summer Squash And Ricotta Galette

Servings: 6

Ingredients:

- 1 medium zucchini, cut into ¼-inch thick slices
- 1 medium yellow squash, cut into ¼-inch thick slices
- 1 medium Mexican squash, cut into ¼-inch thick slices
- 2 Roma tomatoes, cut into ¼-inch thick slices
- 1 tablespoon kosher salt, plus more to taste
- ¾ cup ricotta cheese, strained
- 3 cloves garlic, minced
- 2 sprigs thyme, finely chopped
- 2 tablespoons parsley, chopped
- ½ cup grated Parmesan cheese, divided
- ½ teaspoon ground black pepper
- 1 lemon, zested
- 1 sheet premade pie crust
- 1 egg, beaten, for egg wash

Directions:

1. Lay the squashes and tomatoes onto a wire rack in a single layer and sprinkle with salt to draw out the moisture.
2. Mix the ricotta cheese, garlic, thyme, parsley, ¼ cup Parmesan cheese, ground black pepper and lemon zest in a small bowl. Season with salt to taste.
3. Place pie crust on top of parchment paper for easy removal after baking.
4. Spread the cheese mixture onto the middle of the pie crust, leaving 2 inches of space around the edges.
5. Place the squashes and tomatoes on top of the cheese mixture, alternating between slices.
6. Fold the edges of the pie crust inward, creating a little blanket around the edges to hold everything in place.
7. Brush the edges of the pie crust with egg wash and sprinkle the top with Parmesan cheese.
8. Place the cooking pot into the base of the Smart Indoor Grill.
9. Select the Bake function, adjust temperature 325°F and time to 20 minutes, then press Start/Pause to preheat.
10. Place the galette into the preheated cooking pot, then close the lid.
11. Remove when done, let cool on a wire rack for 5 minutes, then serve.

Air Fryer Edamame

Servings: 4
Cooking Time: 8 Minutes

Ingredients:

- 2 cups fresh edamame or frozen
- 1 tablespoon olive or avocado oil
- 1/2 teaspoon garlic powder
- 1/2 teaspoon kosher salt

Directions:

1. In a medium bowl, toss edamame in olive oil, garlic powder, and salt until well coated.
2. Transfer edamame to the air fryer basket, without stacking or overlapping.
3. Air fry at 400 degrees F for 8-10 minutes, shaking 2 or 3 times during the cooking process so they get an even cook.
4. Remove the basket from the air fryer and allow them to slightly cool prior to eating. Discard edamame pods and enjoy the seeds.

NOTES

Optional Favorite Dipping Sauces: Chili garlic sauce, wasabi and soy sauce, tangy ponzu sauce or siracha or garlic aioli.

Optional Toppings: Toasted sesame seeds, spiced pepitas, a drizzle of reduced balsamic vinegar, sautéed garlic, parmesan cheese, hot sauce or crispy onions.

Substitutions: Sesame oil, refined coconut oil or grapeseed oil.

Cooking Tips: If you are cooking multiple batches place first batches on a baking sheet to evenly cool.

Mother's Luncheon Chicken Salad

Servings: 6
Cooking Time: 14 Minutes

Ingredients:

- 3 thin cut boneless, skinless chicken breasts
- Oil spray, as needed
- ½ tablespoon all-purpose flour (optional)
- 1 teaspoon kosher salt
- ½ teaspoon freshly ground black pepper
- 2 cups green grapes, halved
- 1 green apple, small diced
- 2 celery ribs, small diced
- 1/3 cup plain almonds, roughly chopped
- 2 green onions, finely chopped
- ½ teaspoon freshly ground black pepper
- Herb Dressing
- 3 tablespoons mayonnaise
- 2 tablespoons grapeseed oil
- 2 tablespoons rice wine vinegar
- ½ lemon, juiced
- 1 tablespoon fresh tarragon, finely chopped
- 1 tablespoon fresh chives, finely chopped

- Kosher salt, to taste

Directions:

1. Insert the crisper plate into the Smart Air Fryer basket.
2. Place the chicken breasts in a medium bowl, spray them with oil, then toss them to coat with the salt, pepper, and flour.
3. Place the chicken onto the crisper plate.
4. Select the Chicken function and adjust the time to 14 minutes, then press Start/Pause.
5. Whisk together all of the dressing ingredients in a small bowl, then season to taste with salt.
6. Remove the chicken from the air fryer and let cool to room temperature, then finely dice and toss with the remaining ingredients except the lettuce, and toss enough of the dressing to coat.
7. Serve the chicken mixture on a bed of the lettuce.

Air Fryer Potato Croquettes

Servings: 8
Cooking Time: 15 Minutes

Ingredients:

- 850 g Frozen potato croquette
- Salt to serve optional
- Cooking oil spray

Directions:

1. Preheat the air fryer to 195C/385F for 5 minutes
2. Remove the air fryer basket and spray lightly with cooking oil spray
3. Remove the croquettes from the packaging and arrange them in the air fryer basket in a single layer. Make sure they are not overcrowded but it is ok if they are touching slightly.

4. Cook for 15-18 minutes until crispy and golden brown on the outside flipping the croquettes halfway through the cooking time.

5. Remove the basket from the air fryer, transfer the croquettes to a plate and serve immediately with any dipping sauce of choice.

NOTES

How to store leftovers

Leftover potato croquettes can be stored in an airtight container in the fridge for up to 2 days.

To reheat, preheat your air fryer to 160C/365F and cook the croquettes for 5-7 minutes until heated through. Do not overcook as this will make the croquettes dry out. Do not freeze thawed potato croquette.

Air-fryer Crispy Pork Belly With Mandarin Salad

Servings: 6

Cooking Time: 50 Minutes

Ingredients:

- 1kg pork belly
- 2 tsp sea salt flakes
- 1 tbs Dijon mustard
- 1 tbs Woolworths pure honey
- 1 tbs white wine vinegar
- 1 tbs extra virgin olive oil
- 3 mandarins, peeled, cut crossways thickly sliced
- 60g baby rocket leaves
- 1/2 red onion, thinly sliced into rounds
- 1 fennel bulb, trimmed, thinly sliced

Directions:

1. Preheat air fryer to 200°C. Pat pork dry with paper towels. Rub salt flakes into rind. Line air-fryer basket with foil. Place pork belly, skin-side up, in basket and cook for 30 minutes or until skin is crisp. Reduce heat to 160°C and cook for a further 20 minutes or until pork is cooked through. Rest for 15 minutes. Meanwhile, combine mustard, honey, vinegar and oil in a small bowl. Just before serving, toss mandarin, rocket, onion and fennel in a large bowl.

2. Serve sliced pork with salad drizzled with mustard dressing

Air Fryer Hush Puppies

Servings: 16

Cooking Time: 6 Minutes

Ingredients:

- 1 package of Jiffy Mix (8.5 ounce box)
- 1/4 cup all-purpose flour
- 1/4 teaspoon garlic powder
- 1/3 cup whole milk
- 1 egg
- 2 tablespoons onion, diced
- 1-2 tablespoons jalapeno pepper (or sweet pepper), diced
- OPTIONAL
- pinch of cayenne pepper

Directions:

1. Mix together the Jiffy Mix, flour, garlic powder, and cayenne pepper (if using).

2. Add in the milk and egg and mix to combine.

3. Add the diced onions and peppers and mix to just combine.

4. Preheat the air fryer to 350 degrees and let the mix rest for 5 minutes.

5. Lay down parchment paper rounds* and place drops of hush puppy dough using a cookie scoop or spoon.

6. Cook for about 6 minutes, flipping with 1-2 minutes left.

7. Carefully remove from air fryer and serve.

8. Refrigerate for up to 7 days or freeze for up to 3 months.

NOTES

*must use parchment paper or foil or the mix will stick to the air fryer basket.

To reheat from refrigerated:

Preheat air fryer to 350 degrees and cook for 3-4 minutes until heated thoroughly.

To reheat from frozen:

Preheat air fryer to 350 degrees and cook for 4-5 minutes until heated thoroughly.

Grilled Salad With Raspberry Poppy Seed Dressing

Ingredients:

- 6-8 small-medium hearts of Romaine
- olive oil
- salt & pepper
- Raspberry Poppy Seed Dressing:
- 1/3 cup confectioners' sugar
- ¼ cup raspberry vinegar
- 2 tbsp orange juice
- ½ tsp onion powder
- ¼ tsp salt
- ¼ tsp ground ginger
- 1/3 cup canola oil
- ½ tsp poppy seeds

Directions:

1. In a blender, combine the first six ingredients for the dressing. While blending, gradually add in canola oil until all of the ingredients are blended smooth. Transfer dressing to a mixing bowl and stir in poppy seeds. Refrigerate until ready to serve.

2. Preheat grill to medium high. Brush all romaine halves with olive oil evenly on both sides. Season with salt and pepper to your liking. Place them on the grill and cook for 2-3 minutes per side, or until nicely charred. Drizzle chilled salad dressing on top and enjoy!

Air Fryer Shishito Peppers

Servings: 4
Cooking Time: 6 Minutes

Ingredients:

- 8 ounces shishito peppers, washed and thoroughly dried
- 2 teaspoons olive oil
- 1 tablespoon lemon juice
- ½ teaspoon coarse salt
- ½ cup mayo
- 1 tablespoon lemon juice
- ½ teaspoon paprika
- ¼ teaspoon garlic powder

Directions:

1. Preheat your air fryer to 390 F.

2. Toss peppers with oil in a large bowl until evenly coated.

3. Place in an even layer in the preheated air fryer basket and cook for 6 minutes, shaking the basket halfway through.

4. While the peppers are roasting, prepare a dipping sauce by mixing together the mayo, lemon juice, paprika, and garlic powder until well combined.

5. Transfer the cooked peppers to a platter, drizzle lemon juice over top, and sprinkle with salt.

6. Enjoy immediately with dipping sauce.

Crispy Brussels Sprouts Salad

Servings: 2

Ingredients:

- 200 g Brussel sprouts
- 1 Shallot, sliced
- 15 g fresh mint
- 15 fresh parsley
- 2 tbsp Pomegranate seeds
- 2 tbsp lemon juice
- 2 tsp olive oil
- 1 tsp hot sauce, optional

Directions:

1. Slice the Brussels in half and larger ones in 3. Then add the sliced Brussels and shallot to the air fryer, for around 10 minutes - giving it a shake half way through.

2. To a bowl add the herbs and combine with the oil and lemon juice. Mix through with the crispy sprouts.

3. Add the pomegranate seeds and the hot sauce - if you're using, serve straight away.

VEGETABLE & & VEGETARIAN RECIPES

Air Fryer Potatoes

Servings: 4

Ingredients:

- 1 lb. baby potatoes, halved
- 1 tbsp. extra-virgin olive oil
- 1 tsp. garlic powder
- 1 tsp. Italian seasoning
- 1 tsp. Cajun seasoning (optional)
- Kosher salt
- Freshly ground black pepper
- Lemon wedge, for serving
- Freshly chopped parsley, for garnish

Directions:

1. In a large bowl, toss potatoes with oil, garlic powder, Italian seasoning, and Cajun seasoning, if using. Season with salt and pepper.
2. Place potatoes in basket of air fryer and cook at 400° for 10 minutes. Shake basket and stir potatoes and cook until potatoes are golden and tender, 8 to 10 minutes more.
3. Squeeze lemon juice over cooked potatoes and garnish with parsley before serving.

Vortex Air Fryer Mushroom Stuffed Bell Peppers

Servings: 3
Cooking Time: 17 Minutes

Ingredients:

- 3 large bell peppers
- 1 cup mushrooms sliced
- 1 cup spinach
- 1 cup mozzarella shredded
- 3 eggs

Directions:

1. Preheat the air fryer to 350°F.
2. Cut ¼-inch off the top of the bell pepper and scoop out the seeds.
3. Add the mushrooms and spinach to an air fryer safe pan and cook them until they are tender about 5-6 minutes.
4. Fill the peppers with the mushrooms and spinach, and crack 1 egg into each pepper.
5. Place the peppers in the air-fryer basket and cook for 13-15 minutes or until the egg is cooked. Season with salt & pepper.
6. Sprinkle the mozzarella cheese on top and cook for an additional 2 minutes or until the cheese is melted.

Air Fryer Roasted Potatoes

Servings: 4

Cooking Time: 20 Minutes

Ingredients:

- 1 pound Yukon gold baby potatoes cut into one inch pieces
- 2 Tablespoons olive oil
- 1/2 Tablespoon Italian Seasoning
- 3 cloves garlic minced
- salt and pepper
- 1/4 cup shredded parmesan
- chopped parsley for garnish

Directions:

1. Cut potatoes in quarters using a sharp knife about 1 inch pieces.
2. In a medium sized bowl combine the potatoes, olive oil, Italian seasoning, garlic, salt, pepper and Parmesan Cheese.
3. Add to the basket of your air fryer. Cook at 400 degrees for 10 minutes. Toss the potatoes in the basket and continue to cook for 8-10 minutes or until tender and crisp. Garnish with chopped parsley.

Air Fryer Kung Pao Brussels Sprouts

Servings: 2-4

Ingredients:

- Brussels Sprouts:
- Combine the following in a large bowl:
- 4 cups brussels sprouts, outer layer peeled and quartered
- 2 tbsp extra virgin olive oil like Lucini Italia Premium Select
- 1 tsp garlic powder
- pinch of salt and pepper
- 1/4 cup roasted salted peanuts
- Kung Pao Sauce:
- In a small bowl combine the following:
- 3 tbsp soy sauce
- 1 tbsp honey
- 1 tbsp Sriracha
- 1/2 tsp ginger, grated
- 1/2 tsp garlic, grated
- 1/2 tsp rice wine vinegar
- 1/2 tsp crushed red chili flakes

Directions:

1. Preheat the air fryer to 360 degrees.
2. Mix everything listed under brussels sprouts together except for the peanuts and put in the air fryer for 8 minutes, stopping when there are two minutes left- add in the peanuts and continue to cook for the remaining two minutes. If you like your brussels sprouts crispier, cook for an additional few minutes being careful to not burn them.
3. Once the brussels sprouts are done cooking, remove from the air fryer into the same bowl you mixed

them in-toss them with the Kung Pao sauce and enjoy immediately!

Air Fryer Caprese Stuffed Portobello Mushroom

Servings: 4

Ingredients:

- 1 large clove garlic, grated
- 2 tbsp. extra-virgin olive oil
- 1/2 tsp. kosher salt
- Freshly ground black pepper
- 4 portobello mushrooms (about 1 lb.), stems removed
- 4 oz. low-moisture mozzarella, cut into small pieces (about 3/4 c.), divided
- 8 cherry or grape tomatoes, halved (about 1/2 c.), divided
- Torn fresh basil leaves, balsamic glaze, and crushed red pepper flakes, for serving

Directions:

1. In a small bowl, whisk garlic, oil, 1/2 teaspoon salt, and a few grinds of black pepper to combine. Brush mushrooms all over with oil mixture.
2. In an air-fryer basket, arrange 2 mushrooms domed side up. Cook at 400°, turning domed side down halfway through, until tender, 7 to 9 minutes.
3. Carefully remove air-fryer basket. Fill caps with half of cheese and half of tomatoes; season with salt. Continue to cook at 400° until cheese is melted and golden in spots and tomatoes are softened, 2 to 3 minutes more. Transfer to a plate. Repeat with remaining mushrooms, cheese, and tomatoes.
4. Arrange mushrooms on a platter. Top with basil, a drizzle of balsamic glaze, and red pepper flakes.

Air Fryer Cauliflower

Servings: 2-3

Ingredients:

- 2 tbsp. ghee or butter, melted
- 1/2 tsp. garlic powder
- 1/4 tsp. ground turmeric
- 1 small head of cauliflower cut into small florets
- Kosher salt
- Freshly ground black pepper

Directions:

1. In a small bowl, whisk ghee, garlic powder, and turmeric. Place cauliflower in a large bowl. Pour ghee mixture over cauliflower, tossing to coat until all florets are tinted yellow; generously season with salt and black pepper.
2. In an air-fryer basket, arrange cauliflower in a single layer. Cook at 375°, tossing halfway through, until golden brown, 10 to 12 minutes.

Air Fryer Broccoli

Servings: 2
Cooking Time: 10 Minutes

Ingredients:

- 1 head of broccoli
- 1 tbsp lemon juice
- 1 tbsp olive oil
- ½ tbsp honey Sub with maple syrup
- ½ tsp garlic powder
- ½ tsp red pepper flakes optional
- Salt to taste

Directions:

1. Fill a kettle with water and bring to a boil (this step is optional, only do this if you would prefer to blanch the broccoli)

2. Cut the broccoli in florets, if possible, try and keep them, the same sizes, and transfer them into a bowl. Submerge the broccoli with the hot boiling water and leave for about 30 seconds. Carefully drain the broccoli and run it under cold tap to stop it from cooking.

3. Pat the broccoli dry with a kitchen towel or leave to cool and air dry slightly if time is not of the essence.

4. Place the vegetable in a bowl and season with garlic powder, lemon juice, honey, red pepper flakes salt, black pepper, olive oil, and mix to combine and broccoli is well coated.

5. Transfer the vegetable to the air fryer basket (no need to spray the basket with oil) and cook at 180C/360F and cook for 6 to 10 minutes shaking the basket halfway through for even cooking. Serve immediately with any main meal of choice.

6. Frozen broccoli

7. if cooking from frozen, transfer into the air fryer basket and cook for 1 to 2 minutes just until the veg is thawed. Sprinkle the seasoning on the veggie and mix to combine, spray with cooking oil, stir and spray again so it's well coated. Cook at 190C/390F for 10 to 15 minutes or until crispy around the edges and fork-tender. Serve and enjoy!

NOTES

Add about ⅓ cup of water to the bottom of the air fryer basket to prevent smoking if you would not be blanching the vegetable. This is highly unlikely but if it does then add the water.

Do not overfill the basket when cooking this vegetable otherwise, it wouldn't cook evenly or take longer to cook.

The brand and size of the air fryer you own may affect cooking time. Please adjust accordingly, one of the beauties of an air fryer is that you can easily open it while it is cooking to check for doneness without losing much heat, unlike a conventional oven.

Honey Chipotle Roasted Brussels Sprouts

Servings: 4

Cooking Time: 25 Minutes

Ingredients:

- 1 pound Brussels sprouts
- 2 tablespoons olive oil
- 1/4 teaspoon salt
- 1/4 teaspoon black pepper
- 2 chipotle peppers, from a can of chipotles in adobo
- 1/4 cup honey
- 1 tablespoon adobo sauce, from chipotle can

Directions:

1. Preheat oven to 400°F

2. Prepare the sprouts:

3. Cut Brussels sprouts in half through the end and toss with olive oil, salt, and pepper. Spread out sprouts on an even layer on a baking sheet. Roast for 15 minutes.

4. Prepare the honey-chipotle sauce:

5. Using a small knife, split chipotle peppers in half and remove seeds. Then mince the peppers and add to a small bowl with honey and one tablespoon of adobo sauce from the can.

6. Finish the sprouts:

7. Remove the sprouts from the oven and stir to ensure even cooking, then spread them again into an even single layer on the baking sheet. Toss with the honey chipotle mixture, but reserve a few

tablespoons for finishing the sprouts. Return to oven and bake for another 10 minutes.

8. Serve!

9. Drizzle with the remaining few tablespoons of sauce, and serve sprouts while warm.

Air Fryer Eggplant

Servings: 2-4
Cooking Time: 15 Minutes

Ingredients:

- 1 ounce Parmesan cheese (about 1/2 firmly packed cup grated on a Microplane or 1/3 cup store-bought)
- 1 cup panko breadcrumbs
- 1/2 teaspoon Italian seasoning
- 1/2 teaspoon garlic powder
- 1 large egg
- 1 tablespoon water
- 1 medium eggplant (about 1 pound)
- 3/4 teaspoon kosher salt
- Cooking spray
- Marinara sauce, for dipping

Directions:

1. Heat an air fryer to 400°F. Meanwhile, finely grate 1 ounce Parmesan cheese and place in a shallow bowl. Add 1 cup panko breadcrumbs, 1/2 teaspoon Italian seasoning, and 1/2 teaspoon garlic powder and mix to combine. Whisk 1 large egg and 1 tablespoon water toegether in a second shallow bowl.

2. Trim the stem from 1 medium eggplant. Cut the eggplant crosswise into 1-inch-thick rounds, then cut the rounds into 1-inch-wide fries. Sprinkle with 3/4 teaspoon kosher salt and toss to combine.

3. Working with one at a time, dip each piece of eggplant into the beaten egg and turn to coat. Dredge in the panko mixture, pressing to adhere, and place on a plate.

4. Lightly coat the air fryer basket with cooking spray. Working in batches if needed, place a single layer of fries in the basket (they can be touching but should not be stacked). Air fry for 8 minutes. Flip the fries and air fryer until lightly browned all over, about 7 minutes more. Serve immediately with marinara sauce for dipping.

NOTES

Storage: Store in an airtight container in the refrigerator for up to 4 days. Reheat in a 350°F air fryer until heated through and crispy on the outside, about 5 minutes.

Air Fryer Hasselback Potatoes

Servings: 4
Cooking Time: 40 Minutes

Ingredients:

- 4 medium Russet potatoes
- 4 tbsp olive oil extra virgin
- 1 tsp ground black pepper
- 1/2 tsp kosher salt
- 1 tsp garlic powder
- 1 tsp onion powder
- 2 tbsp parmesan cheese optional
- 1 tbsp parsley chopped, fresh, optional

Directions:

1. Preheat Air Fryer to 350 degrees. Prepare the Air Fryer basket with nonstick cooking spray, olive oil spray, or parchment paper.

2. Slice the potatoes into ¼" sections, careful not to cut all the way through the potato.

3. Add olive oil and seasoning to a small bowl and mix well until combined.

4. Use a pastry brush and brush half of the mixture onto the potatoes.

5. Bake the potatoes at 350 degrees Fahrenheit for 20 minutes. Open the basket and brush the remainder of the mixture to the potatoes and continue to cook for an additional 20 minutes.

6. Remove from the Air Fryer and sprinkle parmesan cheese and fresh parsley before serving.

NOTES

You can reheat Hasselback potatoes in the Air Fryer. Preheat the Air Fryer to 350 degrees Fahrenheit and cook for 5 minutes, or until completely heated through. One of the easiest ways to make sure you don't cut completely through the potato is by using chopsticks on either side of the potato. Slice down to the chopstick and it will serve as the stopping point, keeping you from cutting slices completely through.

Teriyaki Tofu

Servings: 3
Cooking Time: 25 Minutes

Ingredients:
- For The Tofu
- 1 block (250 g) firm tofu drained (see **NOTES**)
- 1-1½ Tbsp cornstarch or arrowroot flour
- ½ tsp onion powder
- ½ tsp garlic powder
- ¼ tsp black pepper
- ½ tsp salt
- For The Sauce
- 3-4 Tbsp maple syrup
- 2 tsp fresh ginger minced
- 1½ tsp fresh garlic minced
- 2½ Tbsp low sodium soy sauce or tamari or coconut aminos
- ½ cup (120 ml) water
- 2 Tbsp lemon juice or rice vinegar
- 1 Tbsp cornstarch or arrowroot flour + 2 Tbsp water
- 2 Tbsp mirin or dry sherry (optional)
- Other Ingredients:
- Cooked rice or rice noodles
- Pan-fried veggies of choice (e.g. red pepper)
- Cooking spray
- Fresh chives chopped
- Sesame seeds

Directions:

1. You can watch the video in the post for visual instructions.

2. Preheat the oven to 400 °F/200 °C and line a baking sheet with parchment paper.

3. Press the tofu for at least 15 minutes. Then cut it into small, bite-sized cubes (about 1-inch) or triangles.

4. To press the tofu, place the block between two layers of paper towels, then place a cutting board on top and something heavy like a cast-iron skillet or several heavy books.

5. Next, combine the cornstarch, onion powder, garlic powder, black pepper, and salt in a medium bowl (or Ziplock bag), add the tofu, and toss to thoroughly coat the tofu.

6. Transfer the tofu to a parchment-lined baking sheet in a single layer. Spray liberally with cooking oil and bake for about 25 minutes, flipping halfway, until the tofu is golden-brown and crispy.

7. Alternatively, air fry the tofu at 400 °F/200 °C for 12-14 minutes, shaking halfway. At the same time, prepare any sides like veggies, noodles, rice, etc.

8. Meanwhile, prepare the sauce by mincing the garlic and ginger, and combine them with the remaining sauce ingredients in a skillet. Bring to a simmer, stirring often.

9. Combine the cornstarch with two tablespoons of water and stir into a lump-free slurry.

10. Add that to the skillet and increase to medium-high heat, constantly stirring, until the sauce thickens. Then, remove it from the heat. Taste test and adjust any ingredients to your liking. i.e., more maple, soy sauce, etc.

11. Add the tofu to the sauce, toss well, and then serve with your side of choice, garnished with sesame seeds and finely chopped scallions or chives. Enjoy!

NOTES

Maple syrup: You can use any other liquid sweetener of choice.

Add veggies of choice: I used peppers because they pair well with this sweet and sour sticky tofu, however, you can use other veggies of choice.

Tofu: If you can't eat tofu because of a soy allergy, I would recommend making my chickpea tofu recipe and adding 1 tsp of agar powder for firmer tofu.

Freeze leftover sauce: You can double the sauce recipe and freeze leftovers. The teriyaki sauce not only tastes great over tofu, but also over roasted veggies!

Air Fryer Blooming Onion

Servings: 4

Cooking Time: 18 Minutes

Ingredients:

- 1 large onion sweet or yellow
- 1 cup all purpose flour
- 1 tablespoon paprika
- 1 teaspoon Italian Seasoning
- 1 tespoon kosher salt
- 1 teapoon garlic powder
- 1 teaspoon chili powder for spicier kick, use cayenne pepper
- 1 cup water
- 1 cup Italian seasoned breadcrumbs

Directions:

1. Because the onion will be very hot, to easily remove the hot onion from the air fryer basket, use a piece of aluminum foil to make an aluminum foil sling for easy lifting.

2. Remove the outer skin of the onion and cut off the top, placing the cut side facing down.

3. Using a cutting board and a sharp knife, slice from the middle of the onion, leaving a small uncut circle in the center. Make 8-10 evenly spaced slices from top to bottom of the entire onion, and through all of the layers, leaving the center connected and root intact to the onion petals.

4. Place onion in ice cold water and let it sit for about 1-2 hours to soften the onion petals to help them separate to coat.

5. In a medium bowl, combine the flour with the spices. Add one cup of water to the dry ingredients, stirring until it forms into a batter. Add one tablespoon of water or extra flour if necessary.

6. Drain onion from the water, patting dry with a paper towel if needed. Open the onion slices, spreading them as much as possible without tearing the center.

7. Place onion in a deep bowl, and dip onion or spoon the batter over the onion, making sure to coat onion sections evenly. Shake of excess batter, and then coat the onion with breadcrumbs.

8. Spray your Air Fryer basket with non-stick cooking spray or line the basket with parchment paper. Place the coated onion cut-side down, in Air Fryer basket.

9. To help your blooming onion crisp, lightly spritz the onion petals with cooking oil spray, and air fry at 380°F for 18-20 minutes until golden brown color with a crispy coating.

Wagyu Sliders With Firecracker Potato Wedges

Servings: 6

Cooking Time: 22 Minutes

Ingredients:

- FOR THE SLIDERS
- 1, 1lb. Sakura American Wagyu Ground Beef Brick
- Autie Nono's Everything Seasoning
- Aged white cheddar cheese
- Arugula
- 6 slider buns
- Kosher dill pickle slices
- FOR THE BALSAMIC CARAMELIZED ONIONS
- 1 yellow onion, thinly sliced
- 1 Tbsp Balsamic vinegar
- 1 Tbsp olive oil
- Salt and pepper, to taste

- FOR THE POTATO WEDGES
- 2 russet potatoes, cut into wedges
- Auntie NoNo's Firecracker Sea Salt
- 1 Tbsp olive oil
- FOR THE FIRECRACKER AIOLI
- ¾ cup mayonnaise
- 1 tsp dijon mustard
- 1 Tbsp lemon juice
- 2 cloves garlic, minced
- 2 Tbsp Auntie NoNo's Firecracker Sea Salt
- 1 tsp paprika

Directions:

1. Combine the aioli ingredients together in a small bowl and placing into the refrigerator.

2. Place the Wagyu beef in a medium sized bowl and season generously with the Auntie NoNo's Everything Seasoning. Form the beef into 6 equal sized slider patties. Press an indention with your finger in the center of each patty to decrease the puffing while cooking. Season both sides of the patties with more Everything Seasoning and set aside.

3. Prep your potato wedges by slicing the russet potato in half lengthwise and then in half lengthwise again. Cut through the center of each to make 4 wedges. We cut each in half, giving us 16 small wedges per potato.

4. Soak the wedges in a bowl with cold water to wash the starch off for about 15 minutes. While the potatoes soak, make your caramelized onions. Heat the olive oil in a pan. Add the onions and the salt and pepper and cook on medium low for about 10 minutes, stirring frequently. Once cooked down a bit, add the balsamic vinegar and cook for another 5 minutes. Set aside.

5. Preheat the 25 Quart Air Fryer Oven using the Grill Preset.

6. Remove from water and dry on a paper towel. In a bowl, combine the potato wedges, 1 Tbsp. olive oil and the Auntie NoNo's Firecracker Sea Salt.

7. Add the potato wedges into the Air Fry Basket accessory and place inside oven near the top. Cook at 450F for 15 min. Shake throughout.

8. Once timer goes off its time to add the sliders to the preheated Grill Tray. Continue cooking at 450F for 4 minutes. Flip and add your slices of white cheddar. Cook for another 2 minutes.

9. Assemble the sliders: Slider bun – slider with cheese – caramelized onions – arugula – slider top bun slathered in the Firecracker aioli – dill pickle slice on top speared with a toothpick. Plate the crispy potato wedges and use the remaining aioli as a fry dipping sauce!

Air Fryer Stuffed Mushrooms

Servings: 4
Cooking Time: 16 Minutes

Ingredients:

- 8 ounces of Italian ground sausage
- 16 ounces of baby portabella mushroom caps
- 2 cups of fresh spinach, chopped
- 2 tomatoes, chopped
- 1/4 cup grated parmesan cheese
- 1 cup of shredded mozzarella

Directions:

1. Brown your Italian sausage over medium-high heat on the stove top. Drain any remaining grease. Set it aside.

2. Chop your tomatoes and spinach. See **NOTES** below.

3. Wash your mushroom caps and remove the stems.

4. Preheat your air fryer to 370 degrees.

5. Combine the sausage, spinach, tomatoes, and parmesan cheese. Using a spoon, stuff each mushroom cap till it is heaping full.

6. You will have to cook two batches of mushrooms, so pair your larger ones in one batch and smaller ones in another to help them cook evenly. Place them in your air fryer basket and cook at 370 degrees: For the larger mushrooms, cook for 5 minutes. Then remove the mushrooms and top them with the shredded mozzarella. Continue cooking for another 3 minutes. For the smaller mushroom caps, cook at 370 for 4 minutes, remove from the air fryer and top with the shredded cheese and cook for another 3 minutes. Allow them to slightly cool and serve.

Air Fryer Moroccan-spiced Carrots

Cooking Time: 2-4 Minutes

Ingredients:

- 1 lb. medium carrots, peeled, trimmed, and cut ½"-thick on the bias
- 1 tbsp. extra-virgin olive oil
- 1/2 tsp. ground cinnamon
- 1/2 tsp. ground coriander
- 1/2 tsp. ground cumin
- 1/2 tsp. kosher salt
- 1/2 tsp. smoked paprika
- 2 tbsp. fresh orange juice
- 2 tsp. fresh lemon juice
- 1/4 c. pomegranate seeds
- 2 tbsp. chopped toasted almonds
- Torn fresh mint leaves, for serving

Directions:

1. In a medium bowl, toss carrots, oil, cinnamon, coriander, cumin, salt, and paprika. Scrape into an air-fryer basket; reserve bowl. Cook at 370° until carrots are just tender, about 13 minutes.

2. In reserved bowl, combine orange juice and lemon juice. Add hot carrots and toss to coat. Top with pomegranate seeds, almonds, and mint.

Air Fryer Potato Wedges

Servings: 4
Cooking Time: 20 Minutes

Ingredients:

- 4 Russet Potatoes
- 2 tbsp olive oil
- 1 tsp paprika
- 1 tsp salt
- 1 tsp garlic powder
- 1/2 tsp black pepper

Directions:

1. To make this recipe, begin by rinsing and then cutting the potatoes into wedges, leaving the potato skin on.

2. In a medium sized bowl, let them soak in cold water for 25-30 minutes. This will remove the starch and makes them crispy potato wedges.

3. After they have soaked, drain water and pat dry with paper towels, and then return them to the bowl.

4. Coat potatoes with a tablespoon olive oil, paprika, salt, garlic powder, and pepper.

5. Next, spread the seasoned potato wedges into the air fryer basket, without overlapping.

6. Return the basket to the air fryer and cook potatoes at 400 degrees F for 20-25 minutes.

7. During the cooking process, shake the basket at the 10 minute mark. If you have larger wedges, you may need to add 2-3 extra minutes for cooking time.

8. Garnish with fresh parsley and serve alone, or with ketchup, ranch dressing, buffalo sauce, or with your favorite sauce of choice.

Air Fryer Fried Green Tomatoes

Servings: 4
Cooking Time: 12 Minutes

Ingredients:

- 2 tomatoes green
- 1/2 cup all purpose flour
- 1 cup breadcrumbs
- 1 cup corn meal
- 2 large eggs whisked
- 1/2 cup buttermilk
- 1/2 teaspoon salt
- 1/2 teaspoon ground black pepper
- 1/2 teaspoon paprika

Directions:

1. Preheat the Air Fryer to 380 degrees Fahrenheit. Prepare the basket with olive oil, avocado oil spray, or nonstick cooking spray.

2. Place the eggs in a small bowl and whisk, and then combine with buttermilk. Add the ground black pepper, salt, and all purpose flour to a rimmed shallow bowl. Add the breadcrumbs and cornmeal mixture to a third bowl.

3. Use a cutting board and a sharp knife to carefully slice the green tomatoes into ¼ inch rounds.

4. Create a dipping station assembly line and dip tomato slices into the flour mixture, then the egg

mixture, and then into the breadcrumb and cornmeal mixture.

5. Place the breaded green tomato slices into a single layer in the air fryer basket. Spray the tops with oil before cooking.

6. Air fry the breaded green tomatoes using the air fryer setting for 10 to 12 minutes, rotating them halfway through the cooking process and spraying the tops again after flipping.

7. When finished, the fried green tomatoes should have a crispy coating and be a beautiful golden brown color.

8. Serve with ranch dressing or your favorite sauce.

NOTES

You can change up the flavor easily with this dish. If you're looking to add additional spice and different flavors, consider adding garlic powder, a little cayenne pepper, and white pepper to the bread crumb mixture.

Additionally, if you want extra crispy tomatoes, consider adding panko bread crumbs to the bread crumb mixture.

For the lower carb version, replace the breadcrumbs, cornmeal, and panko bread crumbs with finely crushed pork rinds. You can use flavored pork rinds for a delicious taste.

This recipe was made with a basket style 5.8 quart Cosori air fryer. All air fryers can cook differently. If you're using a different brand of air fryer, check the recipe during the cooking process to ensure you don't need to slightly adjust the cooking time.

Spicy Sriracha Tofu Rice Bowls

Servings: 2

Cooking Time: 15 Minutes

Ingredients:

- 14 oz extra firm tofu (drained)
- 1 tablespoon plus 2 teaspoons gluten-free Tamari ((or soy sauce) divided)
- 4 teaspoons sriracha (divided)
- 1 tablespoon sesame oil (divided)
- 1 medium scallion (chopped, white and green parts separated)
- 2 teaspoons Thai sweet chili sauce
- For Serving:
- 1 cups cooked brown rice
- 1/2 cup warmed shelled edamame
- 1/2 teaspoon multi color sesame seeds

Directions:

1. Place tofu block between some paper towels and press to absorb extra water.

2. Repeat until tofu feels dry and no more water comes out. Slice across in half lengthwise and then into cubes.

3. In a large bowl stir together 1 tablespoon of the tamari, 2 teaspoons of the sriracha, 2 teaspoons of the sesame and the scallion whites, add the tofu and let sit 10 minutes.

4. Air Fryer Directions:

5. Spray the air fryer basket with oil.

6. Transfer the tofu to the air fryer in a single layer and air fry 370F about 10 to 12 minutes, shaking the basket halfway until slightly golden and crisp on the outside and tender on the inside.

7. Oven Directions:

8. Bake in a preheat oven 400F about 25 minutes, turning halfway.

9. To Finish (air fryer or oven):

10. While it cooks, add the remaining 2 teaspoons sriracha, 2 teaspoons Tamari, 1 teaspoon sesame oil and sweet chili sauce to the bowl.

11. When the tofu is ready, toss it with the sauce to coat until evenly covered. Serve immediately over rice with edamame, sesame seeds and scallion greens.

NOTES

Variations:

Swap the tofu with chicken or shrimp.

If you don't have an air fryer, bake the tofu in the oven at 400 degrees for 25 minutes.

Sub coconut aminos or soy sauce for tamari.

Use plain white sesame seeds or omit them if you can't find multi-colored.

Here, I served these crispy tofu bowls with brown rice and edamame for more protein, but cauliflower rice or stir-fried veggies would also be great.

Vegan Mushroom Jerky

Ingredients:

- 4-6 portabella mushrooms
- 2 tbsp soy sauce
- 3 tbsp apple cider vinegar
- 1 tbsp extra-virgin olive oil
- 1/2 tsp paprika
- 1/4 tsp ground chili powder

Directions:

1. Slice the mushroom into strips approximately 1/4-inch thick

2. Whisk together soy sauce, apple cider vinegar, olive oil, paprika, and chili powder. Transfer to a zip-top bag or airtight container and add mushroom slices. Marinate for 8 hours, up to overnight.

3. Place mushroom slices on air fryer oven racks. Dehydrate for 5 hours at 130° F.

4. Allow jerky to cool completely before transferring to an airtight container. Store jerky in fridge for up to a week. Enjoy!

Air Fryer Frozen Asparagus

Servings: 4

Cooking Time: 10 Minutes

Ingredients:

- 1 pound frozen asparagus
- 1 tablespoon olive oil
- 1 teaspoon garlic powder
- ½ teaspoon kosher salt
- ¼ teaspoon black pepper
- Butter, for serving
- Lemon wedges, for serving

Directions:

1. Preheat your air fryer to 390 degrees F. Spray the inner basket with cooking oil.

2. Place the frozen asparagus in a single layer in the basket - you may need to work in batches. Air fry for 5 minutes.

3. Open the basket and use tongs to transfer the asparagus to a large bowl. Drizzle the oil over, then sprinkle with garlic powder, salt, and pepper. Toss well.

4. Return the asparagus to the basket and air fry for another 3-5 minutes, until fully cooked to your liking.

Printed in Great Britain
by Amazon

29385845R00064